S0-BYT-052

HERESIES AND HERETICS

IS VOLUME
136
OF THE
Twentieth Century Encyclopedia of Catholicism

UNDER SECTION
XIII
OUTSIDE THE CHURCH

IT IS ALSO THE

20TH
VOLUME IN ORDER OF PUBLICATION

Edited by HENRI DANIEL-ROPS *of the Académie Française*

HERESIES AND HERETICS

By MSGR. LÉON CRISTIANI

Translated from the French by RODERICK BRIGHT

HAWTHORN BOOKS · PUBLISHERS · *New York*

273
C 868E

142473

© 1959 by Hawthorn Books, Inc., 70 Fifth Avenue, New York City 11. Copyright under International and Pan-American Copyright Conventions. All rights reserved, including the right to reproduce this book, or portions thereof, in any form, except for the inclusion of brief quotations in a review. This book was manufactured in the United States of America and published simultaneously in Canada by McClelland & Stewart, Ltd., 25 Hollinger Road, Toronto 16. It was originally published in France under the title, *Brève Histoire des Hérésies.* © F. Brouty, J. Fayard et cie, 1956. The Library of Congress has catalogued The Twentieth Century Encyclopedia of Catholicism under card number 58–14327. Library of Congress Catalogue Card No. for this volume 59–6761.

First Edition, June, 1959

NIHIL OBSTAT

Johannes M. T. Barton, S.T.D., L.S.S.

  Censor Deputatus

IMPRIMATUR

E. Morrogh Bernard

  Vicarius Generalis

Westmonasterii, die XVI JANUARII MCMLIX

CONTENTS

CHAPTER I

HERESIES FROM THE BEGINNING TO THE FOURTH CENTURY

WHY HERESIES?

In that sublime prayer, which exegetists call his priestly prayer, Christ asked his Father, as if in anguish, that his disciples might always preserve unity: "Holy Father, keep them true to thy name, thy gift to me, that they may be one, as we are one. . . . It is not only for them that I pray; I pray for those who are to find faith in me through their word; that they may all be one; that they too may be one in us, as thou, Father, art in me, and I in thee; so that the world may come to believe that it is thou who hast sent me" (John 17. 11, 20–2).

He knew, then, the cost and the difficulty of unity which was to be the principal mark of the Church. But there were to be divisions, breaches of unity, divergences of opinion—in a word, heresies. That is in fact the meaning of heresy; the word passed into Latin from the original Greek, and although little used in classical language it was often to be used in the language of the Fathers of the Church.

Whence comes heresy? It springs from the diversity of minds, from personality, from temperament and, ultimately, from the fact of human freedom. Belief in the word of God is free; God compels nobody. But inevitably faith demands an effort of submission and obedience on the part of man; this obedience is a matter of choice, and it is the function of heresies to throw this choice into relief. That is why St Paul could say: "Parties there must needs be among you, so that those who are true metal may be distinguished from the rest" (1 Cor. 2. 19). And Tertullian, a hundred and fifty years later, wrote: "The state of our times compels us to give this warning—you must not be astonished either at the existence of heresies, which was foretold, or that they should destroy the faith of some, for their very purpose is to test the faith of those whom they tempt."

If we try to consider this law that faith needs testing, we observe that it is one of the essential laws governing the mind. The angels were subjected to a test, the nature of which we do not know, but we know it to be a fact by reason of the existence of devils.[1] They were angels as the others were, but they succumbed to the test. Human beings in their turn have to be tested, i.e. tempted. It is easy to see what happens when a heresy arises. We can distinguish three different aspects in the matter of heresy—the philosophical, the paradoxical and the positive. From the philosophical point of view heresy is born of the conflict or contrast between revealed truth and the various philosophical systems already established in the minds of those to whom the revelation is given. Faith does not in fact always light upon minds receptive to it. Christ chose uninstructed apostles who had their own ideas, traditions and conceptions of the messianic kingdom. The Scribes and Pharisees regarded themselves as much more enlightened than the humble fishermen of the Galilean lake. Faith encountered obstacles and had to overcome prejudices amongst all of them. And in passing from Jews to pagans there was an even more acute conflict of philosophical outlooks between faith and the current systems; and so it was to be

[1] See *Who is the Devil?* in the present series.

right to the end of those times. Agreement is not always possible between human philosophies and revealed truth; Christian thinkers have to accomplish a tremendous effort of adaptation between reason and faith.

From the philosophical aspect we come to the paradoxical aspect of heresy, by which we understand that revealed truth, by the very fact of its divine origin, cannot but confront reason with shadows which it will be unable to penetrate. We express this fact when we say that faith comprises mysteries. Reflecting on this we can well understand that a religion without mysteries would not be of divine origin. Faced with faith derived from God, reason must admit its impotence, and it is precisely that which gives heresy its paradoxical aspect, by making reality appear contradictory and paradoxical to the mystery of faith.

Lastly, heresy can be explained in its positive aspect. In reality, not everything about heresy is false; it always contains a legitimate intuition, but this will prove to be warped by the intrusion of a philosophical system contradictory to faith, or by an explicit or implicit denial of the mystery of faith. A rebellion against revealed truth appears in every heresy, and therein lies the fundamental anti-Christian basis of all heresy.

This is the traditional way of interpreting heresy in the Church, but there has always been an insistence on the good which can come from the great evil of heresy, for every heresy has been the occasion of progress in understanding of the faith, and of a strengthening of unity within the Church.

JUDAIZING HERESIES

The oldest known heresy in the history of the Church was that of the Judaizers. It was the obstinate error of those who from the first had opposed the extension of the ranks of the Church so that pagans could enter it *en masse*. These heretics rejected the dogma of the catholicity of the Church.

Jesus had said: "Go out, making disciples of all nations." The Judaizers demanded the retention of the Law of Moses and of all its prescriptions. After veiled opposition, chiefly to the holy daring of St Paul, the Apostle of the Gentiles, the Judaeo-Christians formed separate sects; chief among these was the Church of the Poor—the Ebionites or Poor. Some attempts have been made to connect them with the Essenes, whom the Dead Sea Scrolls have recently made better known to us. The Ebionites seem to have lasted until the fifth century.

GNOSTICISM

As opposed to the Ebionites, who remained too closely attached to their Jewish traditions, the Gnostics were for the most part pagans who, while accepting the Christian faith, claimed to combine with it their own personal ideas, theories, philosophies and ancient myths. The word *gnosis*, of Greek origin, means knowledge or science. The Gnostics regarded themselves as original thinkers who could not conform with the faith of simple believers. During the first centuries of the Church there was a veritable swarm of heresies inspired by Gnosticism. It would serve no useful purpose to enumerate here all the dreamings of these remote sects; a general outline will suffice. The attention of the Gnostics seems to have been attracted to the closely connected problems of creation and evil, for if God created the world, whence did evil come? And if he did not create evil how could he be regarded as the unique author of creation?

The Gnostics constructed daring systems on this theme. In their belief it is necessary to add to the kingdom of light—which is God's kingdom—a kingdom of darkness, composed of eternal matter and darkness. Between the God-Abyss, as they liked to say, and the organizer of matter whom they called the demiurge, they postulated a large number of steps which they called aeons: most of the sects combined a male with a female aeon.

The demiurge, or author of our material world, was either the last of the aeons, according to them, the furthest removed from the unfathomable God, or possibly a demon who had snatched a spark of the divine plenitude—the *Pleroma*—in order to give life to matter.

This theory of the world's origin explains for the Gnostics the diversity of the human mind, and consequently they distinguish between Gnostics or Spirituals (i.e. themselves), ordinary Christians, in whom matter and spirit are almost balanced, and the pagans or Materials (the Hylics), in whom matter is far and away superior to spirit. Applying this theory to the Christian faith the Gnostics made Christ an aeon sent by God. This aeon took possession of the man Jesus in the moment of his baptism in the Jordan. Thenceforth his mission was to lead men to true *gnosis*, which is the pure gospel, in order to release them from matter. Thus redemption is effected through him. When the gospel has done its work on earth all the parts of the divine spirit imprisoned in matter will return to the fullness of God, the divine *Pleroma*, and the kingdom of darkness will remain for ever in darkness.

A certain number of the foregoing ideas have reappeared in our own day among the Theosophists or the Spiritualists. The wonderful intervention of the Holy Spirit was needed to save the primitive Church from being submerged by these bold and pretentious speculations. Gnosticism rendered a providential service to the Church by compelling the faithful to close their ranks around their pastors, particularly the bishop, Christ's representative and successor to the apostles in each local Church.

PRINCIPAL GNOSTIC LEADERS

Gnosticism is usually traced back to that Simon the Magician mentioned in the Acts of the Apostles as having wished to buy the power of making the Holy Ghost come down upon the faithful, as he had seen the apostles do. After him we find a certain Cerinthus who was refuted by the apostles, notably by St John the Evangelist.

But these figures are wrapped in legend. After them the stream of Gnosticism developed in Syria and at Alexandria in Egypt, the former more positive and practical, the latter rather speculative and adventurous. The first of these *gnoses* has but few known names, the second on the other hand had several talented leaders who were refuted by the Fathers, through whom we have been enabled to know their systems. Here it will suffice to name only Valentine, Carpocrates and Marcion.

Valentine, of Egyptian origin, seems to have preached his ideas in Rome between 135 and 160. He was excommunicated several times and driven out of the Church. In the end he withdrew to Cyprus and started a fairly flourishing sect there.

The moral problem seems to have been the chief preoccupation of Carpocrates. There were some among the Gnostics who regarded matter as the seat of all evil and consequently they tried to forbid marriage as impure. They were called the Encratites or Continents. At the opposite extreme Carpocrates and his followers maintained that everything which happens to matter is insignificant as regards the soul. Anticipating Quietism (from which Luther was not to prove exempt; we shall find it asserted by Molinos in the seventeenth century), Carpocrates dismissed all sensual disorders as unimportant. His son, Epiphanes, who died at an early age, ruined by vice, he honoured as a god in his sect. These two, contemporaries of Valentine, are in some measure the forerunners of communism.

Marcion must be considered apart from the other Gnostics. He came originally from Sinope in Pontus, but about 135–40 he reached Rome and contrived his reception into the Church. Ten years later he broke away to found a pernicious sect which managed to exist for a long time. Its fundamental teaching was what he called Antithesis. Rather as Luther did at a later date, it set the Old Testament—the work of the righteous

God—in opposition to the New Testament—the work of the good God. In the same way Luther was to set in opposition the Law, which condemns, and the Gospel, which saves.

THE OPHITES

Among the Gnostic sects was one which worshipped the serpent of paradise, rather as in our own day there are those who worship Satan, prince of this world. They are known by the name of Ophites, or worshippers of the serpent. The reason which they gave for this worship was that, according to Scripture, the serpent was the first to rebel against the demiurge who had created our miserable world, and to give mankind the knowledge of good and evil. This seems to be one of those sects favoured by the apocryphal books, which are only caricatures of the sacred books forming our Bible.

MONTANISM

This abundance of different heresies, not all of which we can enumerate here, testifies to the intense interest that the Christian message aroused in the Greco-Roman world of the second century. Montanism is yet another proof of this interest.

Montanus was born in an Asiatic village in the neighbour-hood of Mycea and Phrygia. He had been profoundly struck by those passages in St John's Gospel referring to the sending by Jesus of the Holy Spirit, and so excited did he become that he reached the point of actually announcing that he was the spokesman of the Holy Spirit promised by Christ, and declaring that a new era and a new revelation were to begin with him. He spoke with the conviction of a madman. "I am come," said he, "not as an angel or messenger, but as God the Father himself. . . . I am the Father, the Son and the Para-clete. . . . Behold, man is as a lyre and I play upon him as with a bow; man sleeps and I arouse him; behold, it is the

Lord who throws men's souls into ecstasy and gives them a heart."

He appeared to be always in a sort of ecstasy. Soon two women, Prisca and Maximilla, were captivated by his teachings and had ecstasies like himself, in the course of which they prophesied. The bishops of the neighbourhood tried to bring them to their senses by canonical exorcism, but in vain. Then the sect was excommunicated, for it was trying to substitute direct inspiration for the authority of the Church.

Montanists particularly professed Millenarianism, an error which maintained that the triumphant Christ would soon come to establish for a thousand years the kingdom foretold in the Apocalypse. The sect, with this Second Coming in view, preached a strict moral rigorism, which led astray even Tertullian, the only notable name which Montanism could boast, although it lasted until the eighth century, especially in the east.

ANTI-TRINITARIAN HERESIES

One of the most imposing dogmas of the Christian religion is that of the Holy Trinity—one God in three Persons.[2] It was inevitable that this doctrine should occasion many speculations and consequently more than one error. The Apologists of the second century vigorously upheld the two tenets of the doctrine, unity of essence and trinity of divine Persons. It was in the course of these definitions that the word Triad or Trinity appeared towards the year 180, at the instance of the Catholic writer, Theophilus of Antioch. But about the same time a very grave heresy, Adoptionism, was born. This consisted in explaining the title "Son of God", given to Christ, by the fact of his adoption by God. Here was a twofold heresy for it rejected the Trinity and denied the divinity of Christ and the Incarnation of the Word. The promoter of Adoptionism was a wealthy leather merchant of Byzantium, Theodotus, who was condemned by Pope Victor I, c. 190. A second Theodotus, a banker, and Artemon became the leading exponents of the heresy.

[2] See *What is the Trinity?* in the present series.

A formidable, scholarly and therefore more serious heresy was spread abroad about the same time. Its originator seems to have been one Noëtus, but he was soon eclipsed by Praxeas. After 210 however, this heresy had as its principal theologian Sabellius, and so it is often called Sabellianism or Monarchianism. The latter name derives from the bold statement of the Sabellians that "we allow only the monarchy", i.e. the unity of person as well as the unity of nature in God. What then were the meanings of the names of Father, Son and Holy Spirit, which had been customary from the earliest times, particularly in the liturgy of baptism? For the Sabellians the three names were merely three aspects or different appellations, but never of distinct persons. So it was the Father who was incarnate in the womb of the Virgin, and who at his birth took the name of Son without ceasing to be the Father. It was the Father, under the name of Son, who preached, suffered and rose again. For this reason orthodox Christians gave the Sabellians the nickname of Patripassians—believers that the Father suffered on the cross for us. They were also nicknamed Modalists because they reduced the three Persons of the Trinity to mere modes of expression.

Generally speaking, Sabellians rejected Adoptionism, but a third-century bishop, Paul of Samosata, managed to profess both heresies simultaneously and was condemned at the Council of Antioch *c.* 268.

PRINCIPAL REFUTATIONS

All the heresies which we have just outlined were the objects of lively refutations by the best writers in the Church. While the Apologists addressed themselves principally to the pagans, the anti-Gnostic or anti-Sabellians described and energetically denounced errors which threatened to overwhelm the Church. We shall confine ourselves to mentioning St Irenaeus, second bishop of Lyons, Tertullian, Origen, St Epiphanius and St Hippolytus. It would be impossible to exaggerate the importance and fruitfulness to the Church of these frequently impassioned controversies. Anything is better for a religion than immobility and inertia. The arguments provoked by men like Valentine, Marcion, Praxeas or Sabellius, or by other heretics, resulted in a consolidation and deepening of Christian doctrine which had constantly to bestir itself and advance against this opposition, as much in the realm of dogma as in the moral sphere. It erred towards neither Encratism nor the laxity of the Quietists. And the Trinitarian doctrine, so profound and mysterious, was defined and ratified with decisive firmness. Indeed, in order to confound the Patripassians more thoroughly the Son came to be distinguished from the Father even to the extent of being declared inferior to and subordinate to the Father. The illustrious Origen himself strayed slightly into this error which is known as Subordinationism, which was to give birth to Arianism in the next century. But it was in the course of these theological researches that a new terminology was evolved which later enabled the most formidable heresies to be refuted.

Tertullian in particular is regarded as the creator of this new language in the west. He produced that excellent formula "three Persons in one only substance". The next chapter will show how the Church made use of this precious formula in a way in which even its author had not always quite understood it.

CHAPTER II

HERESIES IN THE CHURCH IN THE FOURTH CENTURY

ARIUS AND HIS TEACHING

The controversies provoked by anti-Trinitarian errors in the third century had resulted in a very clear condemnation of the Patripassians. But Catholic writers had not always been able to avoid Subordinationism. The popes had certainly never accepted this illogical doctrine. Paul of Samosata had been condemned by the Council of Antioch c. 268 for having made Christ merely an adopted Son of God. It seems that the priest Lucian of Antioch still retained something of this doctrine in the following form: in Jesus the soul which animates man's body was replaced by the Word which can be called God, for he is the first-born of God but is inferior to God since he has been created out of nothing by him. So Lucian of Antioch must very probably be considered the true begetter of Arianism.

Arius was born in Egypt c. 256. He was a priest who had been given the care of a parish in the great city of Alexandria, one of the most important in the Roman empire. He was a large, gaunt man, distinguished, austere, capable and eloquent, very popular in his parish of Baucalis. Moreover, he was ambitious, full of self-importance and very obstinate in his ideas. About the year 318 a doctrinal conflict arose between him and his bishop, Alexander, who, after vainly trying to persuade Arius by gentleness, summoned a council of about one hundred bishops of Egypt and Libya, *c.* 320. This council condemned Arius, who had to leave his parish. He took refuge first in Palestine, then in Asia where he acquired some supporters. He had composed a collection of popular hymns called Thalia, in order to spread his ideas. At Alexandria he had retained certain enthusiastic friends; they sang these hymns against the Catholics, who replied energetically, and only the pagans were entertained by these unfortunate quarrels.

Just about this time the Emperor Constantine had recently triumphed over his rival, Lucius, and re-formed the unity of the Roman Empire under his control. The discussions which were breaking out in Alexandria, Nicomedia, Palestine and Syria were too fierce to escape his attention, and on the advice of Bishop Hosius of Cordova he resolved to summon a general Council to give a final ruling on the teaching of Arius.

This teaching was as follows: God is one and eternal; the Word or Logos is his first creature, having been created by him out of nothing; he made use of him to create our world. Therefore, the Word is superior to and older than all other created things but he cannot be called God save in so far as he is Creator of the world. In fact he is only an adopted son of God. The Holy Spirit in his turn is the first creature of the Son and is therefore inferior to him. It was the Word that came to animate the body of Jesus, born of the Virgin Mary. That is why St John says "the Word was made flesh" and not "was made man". In Jesus the Word replaces the human soul and its function.

The Council of Nicaea, convened at the Emperor Constantine's behest in 325, adopted the term "consubstantial" in order to confirm categorically the perfect equality of the Word with the Father. This was done through the influence of Athanasius, a deacon, chief theologian to the bishop of Alexandria, where the Arian heresy had first seen the light. Only two bishops refused to sign the confession of faith which we call the Nicene Creed,[1] which the council then agreed upon. All the supporters of Arius were deposed and exiled.

ARIANISM UNDER CONSTANTINE

But Constantine did not remain a firm upholder of the doctrine defined at Nicaea. His sister Constantia, who was more or less won over to Arianism, pressed him to recall from exile Bishop Eusebius of Nicomedia, who very soon gained his confidence. Eusebius induced him to believe that the word "consubstantial" savoured of Sabellianism and that it removed all real distinction between the Father and the Son. Thanks to these equivocations Arius was recalled from exile c. 329 or 330, after issuing a very inadequate confession of faith. Pure Arianism found a way of assuming attenuated forms and dragged on for a long time from one form of creed to another, without reaching a precise solution.

Meanwhile, the name of Athanasius became the embodiment of orthodoxy. He had succeeded his bishop at Alexandria in 328, and it was against him that the friends of Arius and Eusebius of Nicomedia concentrated their efforts. They tried to get rid of him. Since Arius had subscribed to an imperfect formula which passed for orthodoxy, the emperor called upon Athanasius to reinstate him and give him back his parish. When he refused, Athanasius was brought before a Council at Tyre and by means of intrigues was himself condemned in 335. In the following year Constantine exiled him to Trier in the heart of Gaul. Meanwhile, we are told that Arius died at the age of ninety, in the midst of the triumph which his friends were arranging at Constantinople to celebrate his re-admission to Catholic communion.

[1] This is substantially the Creed which we sing at Mass; it was completed at the Council of Constantinople in 381.

PHOTINIANISM

To add to the confusion of ideas Marcellus, bishop of Ancyra, published a work directed against Arianism, *c.* 335.

In his anti-heretical zeal he appeared to revert to the error of Sabellius by not making a clear distinction between the three Persons of the Trinity. The Eusebians, who were in high favour with Constantine, seized this opportunity to have Marcellus condemned. The latter protested, and appealed to Pope Julius I, who in 338 and again in 341, declared him to be orthodox. Later on, however, the language of Marcellus of Ancyra was seen to be not entirely satisfactory, and as his ideas had been adopted by Photinus, bishop of Sirmium, the name of Photinianism was given to this heresy which renewed the modalism of Sabellius. All this had inevitably helped to disturb orthodox minds.

SEMI-ARIANISM

Yet some progress had been made towards truth. Arianism was obliged to modify its formulas in order to render them acceptable. Orthodoxy, always valiantly defended by Athanasius and supported by Rome, gained ground. But at Constantine's death in 337 the empire was divided between his three sons, one, Constantius, eventually inheriting from the others. He had theological pretensions and, like his father, fell under the influence of Eusebius of Nicomedia, who may be regarded as the great champion of Semi-Arianism. While Julius I stoutly defended Athanasius, who had first been recalled from exile and then again driven from his see, Eusebius pretended to condemn Marcellus of Ancyra at a council in Antioch in 341, for renewed Sabellianism, but in so doing adopted a Semi-Arian formulary.

At this time Constantius was not yet the sole emperor; his brother Constant was reigning in the west. With the approval of Julius I he convened a council at Sardica—now Sofia in Bulgaria—in which Athanasius took part and over which the aged Hosius of Cordova presided as the papal representative. In spite of opposition from the Eusebians who withdrew at an early stage, orthodoxy triumphed, Athanasius was completely rehabilitated and in 346 was able to return once more to Alexandria.

In the preceding year the west had witnessed the final unmasking of the pernicious and obscure teaching of Photinus of Sirmium, and so of the even more involved doctrine of his master, Marcellus of Ancyra. This doctrine had been explicitly condemned at the Council of Milan in 345, a decision which had helped to clear the air. Thanks to the energetic Emperor Constant it was possible to hope for peace in the Church, but he was assassinated in 350 so that Constantius remained sole master of the Empire. Eusebius of Nicomedia was dead, but two bishops, Basil of Ancyra and Acacius of Caesarea, whose teaching had been condemned at the Council of Sardica in 343, were successful in currying favour with Constantius. Under the influence of Basil who was a Semi-Arian like Eusebius, a whole series of councils was convened, allegedly to put an end to the heresy of Photinus.[2]

It was maintained that the doctrine of Athanasius in which he held that the Word is consubstantial with the Father was no more than Photinianism in disguise. And as it was particularly in the west that the Athanasian teaching and formula were upheld, the emperor, urged by his Semi-Arian advisers, promoted innumerable councils in Italy and Gaul, with the object of destroying the so-called heresy of the Nicenes or supporters of the Council of Nicaea of 325.

These councils were those of Milan in 355, Arles in 353,

[2] Photinus in fact held that the Word, eternally hidden in the bosom of the Father, was only a sort of projection of the thought of God at the moment of creation. According to him, without creation and outside it, no distinction existed between the Father and the Son.

Béziers in 356, etc. Bishops were everywhere constrained to choose between the condemnation of Athanasius or exile. Pope Liberiûs, the successor of Julius I in 352, allowed himself to be outmanœuvred. Unwilling to abandon the cause of Athanasius, he was first exiled from Rome to Beroea (at the end of 355), being replaced by an anti-pope named Felix (355–365); finally he signed a dubious formula which will be discussed later.

Among the most illustrious exiles of this strangely turbulent epoch, mention should be made of two saints much venerated in the west, St Eusebius of Vercelli, and St Hilary of Poitiers, as well as of Athanasius himself, Pope Liberius, and the nonagenarian Hosius of Cordova, who was born in 258. He had been bishop since 295, and was now nearly a hundred years old.

VARIETIES OF SEMI-ARIANISM

What was now to replace the doctrine defined at Nicaea, and what could be substituted for the "consubstantial" of Athanasius? As in our own day, the characteristics of heresy are its variations and fluctuations; in quite recent times Newman observed that departure from orthodoxy entails falling into inconsistency. The Semi-Arians were continually drawing up fresh formulas; they did not want "consubstantial" on the grounds that it savoured of Sabellianism, so they sought for another adjective. With Basil of Ancyra, the true Semi-Arians adhered to the term "similar in substance", *homoiousios* in Greek, rather than *homoousios* which was Athanasius' word. So they were called Homoiousians. At the other extreme of opinion were the pure Arians, who maintained that the Word was "dissimilar"—*anomoios*—from the Father, and they were known as Anomoeans. Finally, between these two opinions was insinuated the view of the fearless Acacius of Caesarea, which suggested that it was necessary only to state that the Word is similar—*homoios*—to the Father, without specifying similarity of substance. These holding this view were therefore known as Homoeans.

The differences which appeared in what are called the four formulas of Sirmium (351–9) make clear the divergences which were then exercising the minds of churchmen. Sirmium, which can be identified with the modern Mitrovitza on the Save in Jugo-Slavia, was the usual residence of Constantius, and it was in this town and in his presence that the ever changing statements of belief were worked out.

The first formula of Sirmium, drawn up under the influence of Basil of Ancyra, is Semi-Arian but could be interpreted in an orthodox manner. The second formula marks the transient influence of the Anomoeans and the declining influence of Basil; this was in the year 357, six years later than the first one. It proclaimed the Son inferior to the Father, and the Holy Spirit inferior to the Son. A shameful attempt by violent means was made to force the aged Hosius of Cordova to subscribe to this formula, but in vain, for he could never be induced to condemn his friend Athanasius. He was then ninety-nine. Since 358 Basil had resumed the offensive and had succeeded in obtaining the emperor's consent to a third formula, in which the orthodox term "consubstantial", decreed at Nicaea, was not to be encountered, but which was none the less capable of a Catholic interpretation. It must be acknowledged that even certain writers of unimpeachable orthodoxy, such as Cyril of Jerusalem, were somewhat apprehensive of this term "consubstantial", as possibly conducive to Sabellianism. Therefore it is not surprising that Liberius— still languishing at Beroea after three years, and seeing his Church at Rome devastated by schism at the hands of an anti-pope—should find himself able to subscribe to this formula in order to regain his freedom. Still more regrettably, he agreed to condemn Athanasius for using this term "consubstantial". However, there is no reason to believe that in so doing the pope himself fell into the heresy, though this has frequently been alleged in the course of discussions about papal infallibility. Liberius lacked clear-sightedness and strength, but his orthodoxy seems to have remained completely intact.

The success of Basil of Ancyra, author of this third formula of Sirmium, was short-lived, for his enemies and rivals extracted a fourth formula from the feeble and pretentious emperor. This declared that the Word was merely like the Father, which represented a victory for the Homoeans over the Homoiousians. Out of prudence, in 359 this formula was signed by the Anomoeans and by Basil himself, who interpreted it in accordance with his personal opinion.

But at this point the Church was involved in a real tragedy. The emperor demanded that all the bishops of the empire should sign this fourth formula, and in 359 he summoned two councils for the purpose, at Seleucia for the east, and at Rimini for the west. At the latter there were four hundred bishops, some eighty of whom were opposed to the Nicene definition. Therefore the majority decided to abide by the Council of Nicaea and to reject the formula of Sirmium. However, the minority employed such guile and caused the emperor to intervene with such severity that, under pain of the direst threats, combined with explanations aimed at quietening consciences, the Fathers were induced not only to sign this formula of Sirmium but also to aggravate the offence. According to the formula, the Word was "like the Father in all things", but at Rimini these last three words were suppressed. In any case, it is certain that the Council of Rimini finally adopted the formula as a result of a complete misunderstanding.

At Seleucia it was the same story. Basil of Ancyra at first argued in his best style; then the emperor's authority turned the scale in the opposite direction. The formula called "homoean", which had been agreed at Rimini, was also accepted at Seleucia, whence it spread to the barbarians who invaded the Roman empire in the following century. When history relates that these people, namely the Burgundians or the Goths, were Arians, it implies that they professed the confession of faith agreed upon at Rimini and Seleucia. In the next year, 360, the Acacians (or Homoeans) managed to triumph at the Council of Constantinople which at that time condemned the terms "consubstantial" (orthodox), "like in substance" (Basil of Ancyra—Semi-Arian), and "unlike" (pure Arian).

It seemed as though heresy had triumphed in the Church. St Jerome, speaking of this short period which ended with the death of the emperor in 361, made a well-remembered comment: "The universe is groaning in amazement at seeing itself become Arian."

But it was not really so. Minds that had so often been deceived by the intrigues and persecution of the court were about to re-assert themselves.

THE TRIUMPH OF ORTHODOXY

On the death of Constantius, one of his nephews, Julian, known to history as the Apostate, assumed power. He had secretly embraced paganism and fallen out with his uncle the emperor following a revolt of the army, which proclaimed him Augustus. Constantius died while marching against him. Now that Julian was master of the empire he sought to re-establish paganism, and his first act was to send back all the exiled bishops to their dioceses, doubtless hoping that this would provoke divisions in the fold of the Church.

We shall not describe here his efforts to revive the now outmoded and enfeebled paganism. He did not pursue this course for long, for in 363 he perished, at the age of thirty-two, during an expedition against the Persians. His successors, Jovian, Valentinian, Gratian, and in particular Theodosius, showed a wide tolerance, remaining aloof from theological discussions or showing a marked bias towards orthodox Catholicism. Only one, Valens, brother of Valentinian I, with whom he shared the empire, posed as the champion of Arianism, as Constantius had done, but without producing any serious disorders in the Church of the east, in which such spirits as Basil of Caesarea and his friend Gregory Nazianzen were then outstanding.

Athanasius before his death was able to contribute towards the pacifying of men's minds. Returning with the others in 362 to his church in Alexandria, he convened a council at which he displayed great breadth of mind in settling all dogmatic differences. He simply revived the decrees of the Council of Nicaea of 325, and refused to permit any quibbling over words. When he died (in his bed) on May 2nd, 373, he had completed one of the most noble tasks which can fall to the lot of a shepherd of souls, for he had established peace in the unity of faith.

Amongst those who followed his example we must note St Hilary of Poitiers in Gaul, St Eusebius of Vercelli in Italy, and those who are known as the Three Cappadocians, Basil of Caesarea, Gregory Nazianzen and Gregory of Nyssa, brother of Basil and possibly the most learned of the three.

THE MACEDONIANS

For almost the whole of the fourth century, which was one of the most brilliant in the story of the Church, the divinity of the Word was under discussion, but there was a tendency to lose sight of the divinity of the Holy Spirit. It is clear nevertheless that those who rejected the consubstantial divinity of the Son rejected with even greater reason that of the Holy Spirit, whom all recognized as occupying the third rank among the "divine Persons". It was not until c. 360 that this question came clearly to the fore. The person of the Holy Spirit was in fact always associated with the other two, especially in the baptismal liturgy. Most Semi-Arians, and above all, pure Arians, declared against the divinity of the Holy Spirit. For this reason they were called the *Pneumatomachi*, which means opponents of the Spirit; they were also known as Macedonians, from the name of Macedonius, bishop of Constantinople, their principal leader, who was deprived of his see in 360 for another reason. This new dispute had the effect of forcing men's minds to envisage the dogma of the Trinity in all its fullness. It was the glory of the great emperor Theodosius that he put a final stop to these harassing controversies, in the course of which, nevertheless, the theology of the Trinity had maintained a remarkable stability. Theodosius, ever since his baptism, received as an adult, had expressed the wish to conform in all things, particularly in the matter of the Trinity, with the opinions of the bishop of Rome and with the faith publicly professed by the pope and by Athanasius of Alexandria. But having become emperor he appreciated that the orientals entertained some susceptibility with regard to the pope and to the successor of Athanasius. Skilfully he summoned a council at Constantinople comprising scarcely any but orientals. Gregory Nazianzen, a great orator, theologian and a true saint, had recently become bishop of that city. The emperor began by restoring to the Catholics all the churches of the city which had been occupied by Arians. Then, in agreement with Gregory Nazianzen, he summoned the eastern bishops, one hundred and eighty-six of whom came, thirty-six of these being Macedonians. The council was presided over successively by Meletius of Antioch, by St Gregory Nazianzen, and after the resignation of the latter by his successor Nectarius. This council definitely approved the doctrines of the Council of Nicaea, hurled an anathema against Arianism and Semi-Arianism, particularly the heresies of the Anomoeans and Homoeans, as well as the Homoiousians. Lastly, the council proclaimed the divinity of the Holy Spirit as equal with that of the Word and of the Father. The Macedonians were thus rejected from the Church and so the Creed of Nicaea was completed; Arianism survived until the seventh century only amongst the barbarians.

CHAPTER III

HERESIES IN THE WEST

GENERAL CHARACTERISTICS

In passing from the east to the west it is impossible not to notice a profound difference between the heresies which were native to these regions. The great heresies of the fourth century revealed themselves chiefly in the east, but they undoubtedly had repercussions in the west. The see of Rome in particular always had something to say in determining Catholic teaching in the face of each heresy, but all the leaders of sects were eastern. The heresies with which we are concerned in this chapter arose in the west. They assumed an entirely different character. The eastern genius tended essentially, and often passionately, towards great metaphysical problems—the Trinity, the divinity of the Word and of the Holy Spirit, the creation of the world and the origin of evil—and this same trend is almost always apparent, as is seen by the question of the hypostatic union of the two natures in Jesus Christ, of the union of the human and the divine wills in him, etc., discussed later. It might be said that the Greek genius tends to an objective view, while the western mind shows a subjective preference: man, human freedom, grace, predestination, faith and works, the evil within us. The Greeks showed themselves enamoured of high metaphysics and the Latins of profound psychology.

This distinction should not be pressed too far, however. The Latins did not in fact hesitate to follow the Greeks in their lofty speculations, and treatises on the Trinity or on the Incarnation were no less in evidence in the west than in the east, but the initiative did not come from the former. On the other hand, the problem of grace as it is bound up with human freedom has been explored much more profoundly in the west than in the east. In the light of these observations we come now to a review of western heresies.

THE DONATIST SCHISM

Use of the term schism, in connection with African Donatism does not imply that underlying the whole discussion there was not a clear case of heresy. The schism arose on the occasion of the election of Caecilian to the archbishopric of Carthage. A party was formed in opposition to him, and it was alleged that his consecration by Bishop Felix of Aptunga was invalid. In fact it was said that Felix had delivered the Holy Scriptures to the state officials at the time of the persecution. That he had been a *traditor*,[1] as was alleged, removed for ever his power to consecrate validly. This theory was somewhat akin to the error of St Cyprian, bishop of Carthage, who had asserted—contrary to the opinion of Rome—that baptism conferred by heretics is invalid. The opponents of Caecilian, in fact, invoked the authority of Cyprian; their leader was a certain Donatus, bishop of Casae Nigrae in Africa, and their leading theologian was another Donatus, nicknamed the Great, hence the appellation of Donatists. They easily found supporters in a country like Africa where tempers are quick and malcontents against Roman domination abounded. The Donatists even had shock troops, as we say today, in the form of fanatical bands of men who called themselves the soldiers of Christ, but whom the Catholics nicknamed Circumcellions.[2]

[1] One who instead of hiding the Scriptures delivered them (*tradere* in Latin means "to deliver"—hence *traditor*) to the persecuting authority.

[2] *Circumcellions*, because, in need of food, they wandered around (*circum*) the huts (*cellae*) of the agricultural labourers, begging bread.

Doctrinally the Donatists professed two equally heretical principles; (1) public and open sinners, especially treacherous bishops and priests (he who was a *traditor*), no longer belong to the Church; and (2) all sacraments outside the true Church are invalid.

What was even more serious was the Donatists' claim to drive out of the Church not only bishops and priests whom they accused of being traitors, but also the faithful who remained in communion with them. Thus they came to consider themselves the only true Church. All the rest of the Church, according to their belief, was outside Christian truth. How far removed was this attitude from the spirit of mercy which permeates the Gospel. So dangerous and radical a heresy had to be vigorously resisted by Catholics. Donatism was in fact condemned at the Council of the Lateran at Rome in 313, and again at the Council of Arles in 314, at which the emperor Constantine presided. Henceforth all the emperors, with the single exception of Julian the Apostate, were rigorously opposed to Donatism but were powerless to uproot it. Political considerations and an African nationalism analogous to that with which we are familiar today influenced men's minds in favour of the sect.

The mighty doctrinal opponent of Donatism in the fifth century was St Augustine, bishop of Hippo. In 411 a great debate took place at a council held in Carthage, at which two hundred and eighty-six Catholic bishops were present, opposed by two hundred and seventy-nine Donatists. There were then two bishops, a Catholic and a Donatist, in almost all the small towns of Africa. As a consequence of the eloquence and biblical knowledge of Augustine the council condemned the schismatics against whom the State took stern measures. Conversions greatly increased and heresy gradually disappeared.

These occasionally violent disputes had a happy issue, for it was established that one does not leave the Church through sin, even mortal and open sin, but only by apostasy from the faith, and that for a sacrament to be valid a state of grace is not a necessary condition in its minister.

PRISCILLIANISM

The Priscillian heresy owed its origin to one Priscillian, bishop of Avila (the future birthplace of St Teresa); he belonged to a noble Spanish family and was well versed in the art of divination, which was very popular at the time and in practice verged on magic. About the year 370 Priscillian had begun to spread ideas of Gnostic and Manichean origin through which he claimed to lead his followers to perfection. He had also gained the confidence of several Spanish bishops and had in this way himself become a bishop. His teaching was however strongly opposed by several orthodox bishops, St Ambrose in Italy and St Martin in Gaul taking part in the controversies to which they gave rise. Priscillian was condemned by several councils and was delivered up to the civil arm, to the great regret of St Martin who thought that heretics should be won over and not put to death. Priscillian's death took place about 385, but he left behind him followers who prolonged, and seemingly even exaggerated, his errors. They can be regarded as the distant forebears of the Albigensians. They practised certain magical arts and believed that man's fate was written in the stars. Two centuries later Gregory the Great was obliged to refute them.

"Let it be known," he wrote, "that the Priscillian heretics think that all men are born under a conjunction of stars, and they claim in support of their error that a new star appeared when our Lord showed himself in the flesh." The Council of Braga solemnly condemned the Priscillians in 565.

ERRORS CONCERNING THE STATE OF VIRGINITY

By mentioning the names of Helvidius, Bonosus, Jovinian and Vigilantius here we are not implying that they provoked any very grave dissensions in the Church. They are scarcely known to us except through the vigorous refutations of St Jerome and some other Fathers. They were all more or less opposed to Christian asceticism, particularly to the ancient practice, as old as the Church, of dedicated virginity. Through the mouth of St Jerome and by the decisions of councils, the Church wished to establish the superiority over the married state of the state of virginity consecrated to God in the religious life, the perpetual virginity of Mary, mother of our Saviour, and the value and merit of Christian asceticism by the practice of fasting, abstinence or in the monastic life, and the lawfulness of devotion to saints and relics. The heretics' denial of all these points was to appear again twelve centuries later in Protestantism. The best known of the objectors appears to have been Jovinian, an Italian, who was condemned in 390 by Pope Siricius at a Roman council, and by St Ambrose at the Council of Milan in 391.

PELAGIUS AND THE PELAGIANS

A much more serious matter was the heresy connected with the name of Pelagius, who was born in England about the year 354, the same year as St Augustine, who was to become his great opponent on the side of orthodoxy. Pelagius seems to have reached Rome in 384; he was a highly talented and virtuous man. An orator, writer, exegetist, he remained an "independent lay doctor", but possibly he had some connection with the teachings of pseudo-Ambrose—the Ambrosiaster —who was inspired by the school of Antioch. Pelagius was certainly in good faith; he seems never to have contemplated creating a schism or founding a sect. His aim was to react against a surface and entirely external religion, such as was evidently being propagated in the mass conversions of pagans to Christianity. He was a prolific writer, but most of his works have perished, though we possess some of his various exegetic works, notably a letter to Demetrias which resembles a course of spiritual instruction.

Pelagius was above all a severe and uncompromising moralist, strict in his own fashion which was quite the reverse of the Jansenists of whom we shall speak later. He preached detachment from riches and the practice of the evangelical counsels of poverty and chastity in all their severity. He strongly opposed all laxity and insisted on heaven and hell as the eternal sanctions of our actions.

In what then does the heresy of such a zealous and upright director of souls consist? In his deformation of grace. He sets before souls a high ideal of justice, or sanctity, but relies chiefly on the individual will to achieve this, on human freedom turned entirely towards God. Of course, even Pelagius could not fail to speak of grace, which is mentioned so frequently in St Paul's writings. But for him grace is simply nature itself, so lavishly endowed by God in creation. While we are indeed grateful to God for his gifts yet we believe that original sin has caused us to lose a large part of them. But Pelagius denies original sin. According to him it is not possible for the soul, created directly by God, to be tainted by a sin which it has not committed. Confronted with the fact of infant baptism, the practice of the Church from the very beginning, Pelagius refused to admit that this baptism removes an original sin in the soul of the recipient. Doubtless baptism effaces sins previously committed by adults but one cannot say that it may be given to infants "for the remission of sins". Its only purpose is to throw open the kingdom of heaven to them, but this kingdom is merely one aspect of eternal life. Children who die unbaptized also go to heaven but not to the "kingdom of heaven", which is only a part thereof.

Nevertheless, Pelagius avoided detailed explanation of this obscure point. Above all else he loved to extol the ability of our freedom of will to choose at pleasure between good and evil, and to fulfil all the divine law by its own strength. His chief follower was the Italian bishop Julian of Eclana, who said in Roman legal parlance: "By freewill man has been emancipated from God." By this he meant that by reason of our freedom we are not slaves. We can say to God "yes or no" at our own choice and at our own risk and peril. So the first duty of man is to become aware of this splendid autonomy and to use it for his complete sanctification.

The teaching of Pelagius had the appearance of greatness, which explains the large number of people whom it successfully deceived; it magnified the human will. In certain Roman circles where Stoicism still survived it was impossible not to applaud these appeals to human action. Pelagius seems to have preached in Italy freely and without contradiction until the year 410, at which date a great disaster occurred. Everywhere the Roman frontiers gave way to the pressure of barbarian invaders. Bands of Visigoths, led by Alaric, spread from the north into Italy and soon reached Rome. The eternal city, as it was already called, was taken and ruthlessly pillaged. Men thought that the end of the world had come. The distracted population fled from the advancing barbarians, a sight which has been seen again in our own day in all its horror. Pelagius and his principal Roman disciple, the young lawyer Celestius, were among the refugees. They went first to Africa, but while Pelagius set out for Palestine where he received a favourable enough welcome, Celestius provoked objections, criticism and justifiable opposition. A council met at Carthage in 411, condemned his teachings and excommunicated him. He appealed to Rome, but instead of going to the pope to follow up his appeal, he fled to Ephesus where he contrived to be ordained priest. In Africa, however, the struggle against his teachings continued, St Augustine being at the centre of it. The latter wrote several works in succession against Pelagianism—"Of the Spirit and the letter"[3] in 412, "Of Nature and Grace"[4] in 415, and several others. It was then that he earned the title, by which he is known to us, of "the doctor of grace". None knew better than he how to extract from the Scriptures and from tradition the teaching of the Church on original sin, on the necessity of baptism for salvation, and on the prevenient

[3] *De Spiritu et littera.*   [4] *De natura et gratia.*

and auxiliary action of grace in the work of our salvation. Pelagianism, at first misunderstood in the east, and declared orthodox at the councils of Jerusalem and Diospolis in 415, was ceaselessly condemned by the African councils approved by Rome. In spite of the clever tactics of the Pelagians, who defended themselves by every sort of sophism, Pope Zosimus, though persuaded temporarily of Pelagian orthodoxy, eventually hurled an anathema at this pernicious and subtle heresy in an encyclical called *Epistola tractoria*, in the summer of 418. There still remained eighteen Italian bishops, of whom the best-known is Julian of Eclana, who refused to subscribe to the doctrine defined by the pope. But they were vehemently refuted and the heresy disappeared relatively quickly.

SEMI-PELAGIANISM

All the arguments with which St Augustine opposed Pelagianism had been drawn from the Gospels and from the Epistles of St Paul. He had had no difficulty in demonstrating that the very foundations of the Christian faith were affected, for Pelagianism tended quite simply to prove the inutility of Christ, which was later to be the Jansenists' great argument. Without original sin there is no need for a redeemer; prayer is useless if we are sufficient in ourselves.

Christ had said: "No one comes to me unless my Father calls him." And St Paul asked: "What have you that you have not received, and if you have received, why glorify yourself as if you had not received?" Such was the force of these texts that Pelagianism was powerless before them. But monks in the south of France took offence at St Augustine's vigorous expressions about the need of grace; they believed that allowance was not made for the part played by freewill in the work of salvation. Their spokesman was the famous author of the *Conferences*, John Cassian, founder of the monastery of St Victor of Marseilles. He freely admitted the need for grace and recommended prayer, indeed unceasing prayer; but in his

thirteenth Conference he attributed to the ascetics and pious
spiritual writers of the Egyptian deserts, whom he had known
well and consulted, the following doctrine: (1) It is in man's
power to turn first towards God just as it is in a sick man's
power to call first upon the help of his doctor; (2) so eternal
predestination depends in the last analysis on the human will,
for it is this which must persevere until the end. In other
words, John Cassian rejected prevenient grace and the grace
of final perseverance.

Informed by one of his disciples, St Prosper of Aquitaine,
St Augustine at once wrote two works on this question in
which he refuted what came to be called the "Error of the
Marseillais", but which we have known since the seventeenth
century as Semi-Pelagianism. He insisted on the words of
Christ: "Separated from me you have no power to do anything", and on the other texts quoted above. After Augustine's
death on August 28th, 430, his teaching was ratified by an
encyclical of Pope Celestine I to the bishops of Gaul. This
did not condemn individuals. The ideas of Cassian were upheld by a noted writer, St Vincent of Lérins, and by a zealous
bishop, Faustus of Riez. But the doctrine of Augustine also
made its way in Gaul and finally two great bishops of Gaul,
St Caesarius of Arles and St Avitus of Vienne, ensured the
positive condemnation of Semi-Pelagianism at the Council of
Orange in 529. Boniface II solemnly approved the decrees
of this council in 532, which laid down that man, fallen
through original sin, can neither obtain faith nor even desire
it without prevenient grace. Nor can he persevere in good
without a series of auxiliary graces, nor yet persevere until
the end without a special gift attached to his predestination.

Here were some very serious and difficult questions. One
wonders whether St Augustine, in his zeal to refer all the
work of salvation to God and in his steady insistence on the
need for predestination, has not sometimes opened the way
to doctrines leading to fatalism. He is indeed constantly
invoked by the predestinationists. It had been necessary, in

fact, to condemn the priest Lucidus for his teaching on this subject. Luther, Calvin, Baïus, and Jansenius all claimed to shelter under the mighty name of Augustine, and the Church was obliged to interpret Augustinian thought in a manner capable of reconciling the rights of human freedom with the action of divine grace. As always, Catholic doctrine has had to evolve and to adhere to a path between two equally false extremes. But some great controversies (notably between Thomism and Molinism) were to arise on this point which will doubtless never be decided. Bossuet's saying: "Let us hold fast to both ends of the chain" remains a wise one.

CHAPTER IV

CHRISTOLOGICAL ERRORS FROM THE FOURTH TO THE SEVENTH CENTURIES

APOLLINARIANISM

On returning to the east from the west we again encounter speculative controversies. The disputes are less concerned with grace and human freedom than with the nature of Christ, and the union in him of the human and the divine nature. Fresh doctrinal deviations always appear in close connection with the Arian and Semi-Arian heresies.

We have seen, for example, that according to Arius the soul of Christ was none other than the Word, the first creature brought out of nothing by God. Once more we encounter something similar with Bishop Apollinarius of Laodicea. He was a learned and virtuous man who had shown himself resolutely opposed to Arianism by upholding the divinity of the Word or Logos. But he was unable to avoid falling into the same error as Arius concerning the soul of Christ. For him, as for Arius, it is the Word that holds the place of that soul and, again with Arius, he interprets the words of the Gospel "and the Word was made flesh" (John 1. 14) in that sense. He believed that thereby he could better safeguard the unity of person in Christ, and especially his perfect holiness, for he said that where there is complete man there is also sin.

Apollinarianism was however rejected by several councils, notably by the great Council of Constantinople in 381.[1]

NESTORIUS AND NESTORIANISM

In order to fight Apollinarianism more thoroughly, Diodorus, bishop of Tarsus since 378, and principal doctor of the school of Antioch, had tended to substitute "Son of God, consubstantial with the Father" for "Son of David, born of the Virgin". The son of David, according to him, had been only the temple of the Son of God. Thus Mary in no way deserved the title of Mother of God. Diodorus, an excellent bishop and theologian, thought thus to safeguard the moral unity of Christ, but he did not realize that he was doing so only in words. Indeed, he really seemed to be admitting two persons in the same Christ, a divine person and a human person. After the death of Diodorus in 394, his chief follower, Theodore, bishop of Mopsuestia since 392, tried to penetrate what we should today call the human psychology of Christ. He saw him developing like any other man, struggling as we do against temptation but in the end meriting his union with the Word. Yet Theodore was careful to clothe his idea in such a traditional form that it gave rise to no objections. However, in the very year in which Theodore died one of his followers, the priest Anastasius whom Nestorius, the new bishop of Constantinople, had brought thither from Antioch, based his preaching on these ideas. When speaking in public of the Virgin Mary he disputed the right of Christian people to call her the Mother of God—*Theotokos*—as had been the established custom. This view of Anastasius caused a stir in the city; to the astonishment of the faithful, Nestorius,

---

[1] Although this council was only composed of eastern bishops and was not presided over by a papal legate, it ranks amongst ecumenical councils since it subsequently received the approval of Rome and, with Rome, of the whole Church.

who shared Anastasius' conviction, following Diodorus of Tarsus and Theodore of Mopsuestia, took his part and spoke in his support. A layman named Eusebius, who shortly afterwards became bishop of Dorylaeum, protested strongly against the bishop's language. The whole city and the court were amazed. The imperial court took the bishop's side, but the monks and the laity adhered to the Marian tradition. Soon the din of these arguments reached Alexandria, the episcopal see in traditional rivalry with the school of Antioch and the see of Constantinople. Cyril, the bishop of Alexandria and a theologian of the first rank, quickly intervened, courteously at first writing personally to Nestorius. Then, when he saw that his intervention was being ill-received, he referred the matter to Rome. Nestorius had already done so.

On all sides it was perfectly well understood that the crux of the problem was in the use of the title "Mother of God" applied to Mary. If it was not given to her the unity of person in Jesus Christ was impaired. Instead of one person two were implied, the human person of Christ of whom Mary was the mother (*Christotokos*) and the divine person of the Word, superimposed on that of Christ in a purely moral union. If, on the other hand, in accordance with constant Christian tradition, only one person in Christ was admitted, that of the Word, it followed that the relation of motherhood in so far as it affected that person through giving birth to the nature, must include the Word. Mary must be called—inasmuch as she was the source of the human nature of Christ—Mother of God. Motherhood and filiation in fact are said to be from person to person.

So Rome understood the matter; Celestine upheld Cyril against Nestorius. His first deacon, Leo, the future pope, immediately wrote to John Cassian whom he had known for a long time, asking him for a treatise on the subject. Cassian complied with this request and we have his treatise, in which he shows, from Scripture and tradition, that Mary ought not to be called only the Mother of Christ, unless it is made clear that it also implies Mother of God.

If Nestorius refused to accept this conclusion it was not possible to treat him as anything but a heretic, and the matter was serious enough for a general council to be held to consider it as soon as possible. During the interval Cyril summarized his views in twelve anathemas, to which Nestorius replied with twelve counter-anathemas accusing Cyril of relapsing into Apollinarianism by making the Word take the place of the human personality of Christ.

THE COUNCIL OF EPHESUS

The two emperors Theodosius II in the east and Valentinus II in the west had summoned the bishops to Ephesus for June 7th on which date Cyril was present with a number of bishops, but neither the papal legates nor the bishops from Antioch had arrived. Cyril, who was the most important person present, waited patiently for a fortnight during which he carried on skilful negotiations with the court; then on June 22nd he opened the council without further delay, and in one day the dispute was settled, Nestorius being condemned and deposed. The bishops, one hundred and ninety-eight in number, and the people acclaimed these decisions.

Four days later John of Antioch arrived with his own bishops, all of whom favoured Nestorius who belonged, as we have seen, to the school of Antioch. They set up a counter-council to the one held on June 22nd, and condemned Cyril, excommunicating him and annulling everything that had been done in their absence. This was the second act of the drama, but the third was soon to follow. The papal legates arrived shortly afterwards, bringing with them a formal condemnation of Nestorius which Celestine I had pronounced in a Roman synod. They were commissioned by the pope to ask Cyril and the whole council for a straightforward promulgation of the irrevocable judgement already pronounced by the Roman

Pontiff. So on July 11th, 431, they ratified all the decisions taken by Cyril and the council of the preceding June 22nd.

Nestorius, however, was still relying on the support of the imperial court and a diplomatic struggle ensued between Cyril and the court during which he was obliged to resort to a course of action only too usual at that time and heap presents on the most influential advisers of the emperor. In this, he was on the whole justified, for Theodosius II let himself be persuaded. He confined Nestorius in a monastery and permitted Cyril to return triumphantly to Alexandria, while John of Antioch went back greatly discontented to Syria. Cyril was obliged to establish that he had in no way accepted Apollinarianism, and finally peace was restored between him and the bishops of Antioch in 433.

Nestorius was later sent into exile where he wrote a work entitled *The Bazaar of Heracleides* which, discovered *c.* 1895, was first published in 1910 and is a shrewd apologia. But the Nestorian heresy, though disguised, is still clearly to be discerned in it. Even after the writings of Nestorius had been consigned to the flames his heresy continued in the works of Diodorus of Tarsus and Theodore of Mopsuestia. Consequently, it retained adherents and has done so even to our own times. It established a school of theology at Edessa, then at Nisibe in Persia, whence Nestorianism spread to Arabia, India and even China and Mongolia. However, at the beginning of the sixteenth century, the greater part of the Nestorians returned to Catholic unity. Some fell under the influence of protestant missionaries, both Anglican and American, while others after 1897 passed into Russian Orthodoxy. During the First World War a large number were massacred by the Turks. Still others fled into the mountains of Kurdistan, or to Mesopotamia. Nestorians are still found today in Iraq, Syria, Persia and India. It is estimated that there are 30,000 in Iraq, some thousands in Syria, 9,000 in Persia, and 2,000 in India, under the name of Mellusians. Altogether there are certainly less than 100,000 authentic Nestorians.

EUTYCHIANISM

Just as Nestorianism had been a reaction against Apollinarianism so Eutychianism was a reaction against Nestorianism, but is was so extreme that it fell into the opposite error.

We have seen how Cyril of Alexandria was obliged to defend himself against the suspicion of Apollinarianism. In order the better to express the unity of person in Christ he had unfortunately used the term "physical unity" of the humanity and divinity in the single person of the Word. Today we speak of the hypostatic union, which implies union of the two distinct natures in a single person. But, before such precision had been reached, a monk of Constantinople named Eutyches, an archimandrite of a large monastery in that city, attracted attention by his zeal in speaking of the physical union of the human and the divine in Christ, which he did in the conviction that he was being faithful to the mind of Cyril. The latter, who had died in 444, certainly held an orthodox view. Eutyches interpreted him badly, for he seems to have assumed that the humanity of Jesus was absorbed by the divinity and merged in it, like a drop of water in the ocean. The same Eusebius of Dorylaeum who denounced Nestorius, denounced Eutyches to his bishop, Flavian of Constantinople, who procured his condemnation in synod in 448. Eutyches at once appealed to Rome as was the general custom at that time; there St Leo the Great had been governing the Church since 440.

At the same time Eutyches appealed for the assistance of the bishop of Alexandria, Dioscorus, who at once joined forces with him, and also for the support of the emperor who was still Theodosius II. In these circumstances the latter summoned a council, again at Ephesus.

THE COUNCIL OF CHALCEDON, 451

The council which met at Ephesus in 449 was marked by unfortunate violence. It was presided over by Dioscorus of

Alexandria; the papal legate was refused the chief place which was his by right. The one hundred and thirty-five bishops present were constrained by threats of armed force organized by bands of monks won over to his cause by Eutyches, who was one of them, to sign, so to say, a blank cheque for the condemnation of the orthodox doctrine stigmatized under the name of Duophysicism, or two natures in Christ. Flavian of Constantinople was ill-treated and the emperor, who was misled, confirmed the sentence deposing him and sending him into exile, where he died. St Leo, informed of what had occurred by the papal legates who had fortunately escaped, lost no time in stemming the course of this evil. He held a synod at Rome, in accordance with the contemporary papal custom of acting in synod, as later it was to become of acting in consistory. This Roman synod, held in 449, annulled all the proceedings at Ephesus, which the pope described as "that shameful council of robbers"—*latrocinium*—a name which has clung to it as the "robbery of Ephesus".

The death of the emperor Theodosius II hastened the solution of this sorry conflict. He was succeeded on July 28th, 450, by his sister, Pulcheria. With the agreement of her husband Marcian, she summoned a general council which opened at Chalcedon—the modern Kadi-Keui—opposite Constantinople in Asia. This time all passed off properly, with the papal legates presiding. Dioscorus of Alexandria was present but had with him only about twenty Egyptian bishops who were lost in the crowd of between five and six hundred bishops assembled for the council. He was judged and sentenced to be deposed for his conduct at the Council of Ephesus. The true doctrine had been set out in masterly fashion two years previously by St Leo in a letter, which has remained famous, addressed to the patriarch Flavian. It can be reduced to the following points which always form a summary of the Catholic Faith:

(1) There is only one person in Jesus Christ, the person of the Word incarnate in our nature.

(2) In this one person of the Word after the Incarnation there are two natures, the divine and the human, without commingling and without possible confusion.

(3) Each of these two natures retains its own operation which it achieves in communion with the other.

(4) By virtue of this substantial union of the two natures, we must attribute to the Word alone everything which, in Christ, pertains to the Son of God and to the Son of Man. It is in this sense that we are able to say that God died for us.

This attribution to the sole person of the Word of all the human and all the divine in Jesus Christ has been called *communication of idioms*, i.e. the exchange of the properties of each nature.

This letter of St Leo's was received with enthusiasm; the Fathers exclaimed, "Peter has spoken through Leo!" In the confession of faith adopted by the council the Christological doctrine was expressed in these precise terms: "We teach unanimously that there is one only Son, our Lord, perfect in his divinity and perfect in his humanity, truly God and truly man, composed of a reasonable soul and of a body, consubstantial with the Father according to his divinity and consubstantial with us by reason of his humanity, like unto us in all things except sin."

This declaration was subscribed to by three hundred and fifty-five bishops. After the council had finished its dogmatic work the Fathers, despite the opposition of the legates, declared in the famous Canon 28, that the Patriarch of Constantinople should rank second in the Church to the Roman Pontiff. But in ratifying the acts of the council the pope expressly declared in 453 that he was approving and confirming only those decisions which concerned the faith, and not the others.

Unfortunately, the Egyptian bishops did not submit; they considered Eutychianism to be the real teaching of their great doctor St Cyril; this was untrue. Yet Monophysitism (only one nature in God) persisted in Egypt, and the clergy of that country soon fell into open schism. Without recording here in detail the innumerable incidents which marked the controversies between Monophysites and orthodox Catholics, it is sufficient to note that the former succeeded in setting themselves up as a Church. The divisions which broke out among them in the sixth century, as always happens when Roman unity is lost, did not stop them organizing themselves and continuing to exist. The Monophysite Church exists still in Syria, Mesopotamia, Babylonia and Egypt. The groups are, however, independent of one another, the most important being that in Egypt, where it constitutes what is known as the Coptic Church.

THE THREE CHAPTERS

It must not be thought that the Church lost the profound sense of unity which it held from its Founder. On the contrary, every effort was made to reconcile the various Christian parties which the Monophysite controversy set against each other. All that we have to say here fits into the context of that major preoccupation, but it must not be forgotten that a political concern was added to a religious one. The breach of Catholic unity was made more dangerous—as happened in the case of Donatism—by local nationalist passions which tended to divide the empire. It was an Egyptian usurper, Basiliscus, who consolidated Eutychianism (or Monophysitism) at Alexandria *c.* 475. After his downfall, the emperor Zeno, who was ill-advised by the Patriarch Acacius of Constantinople, published a formula for conciliation, called *Henoticon* (or Unification) in 484. But Pope Felix II considered this formula to be insufficient and inadmissible. Acacius proved adamant and broke communion with Rome. This was the Acacian schism which lasted for thirty-five years (484–519); it was successfully healed when the famous emperor Justinian (527–65) came to the throne. He followed the example of many of his predecessors by considering theological questions to be within the province of his government. He allowed himself to be guided very frequently by his clever and spiritual wife, Theodora, who had been a dancer, but who prided herself on her deep knowledge of religion. With the object of flattering the Egyptian Monophysites Justinian summoned a council at Constantinople in 553, which is regarded as the fifth ecumenical council. At this three groups of writings were condemned as being tainted with Nestorianism; they were thenceforth known by the name of the "Three Chapters": (1) the writings of Theodore of Mopsuestia, who died in 428, (2) those of Theodoret of Cyr against St Cyril of Alexandria in the fifth century, (3) a letter of Ibas, bishop of Edessa, a Nestorian leader, addressed to the Persian Maris. These three groups of writings were abhorred by the Monophysites and their condemnation gave them great satisfaction; but they demanded more. According to them, the decisions of the Council of Chalcedon should have been annulled and Monophysitism adopted, but it was impossible to concede this. Pope Vigilius was well aware that the decisions of the council would lead to no successful result, but as they were justified he finally approved them, though not without hesitation.

THE ORIGENIST CONTROVERSY

It was at this same council in 553 that Origenist doctrines were also condemned. At the beginning of the third century Origen had been head of the catechetical school of Alexandria. He was possessed of considerable genius and produced a great number of works. Inevitably, in this mass of writings from his own hand and those of several copyists who wrote at his dictation were to be found more or less dubious doctrines. In those of his works known to us there is something of everything; there are certainly magnificent passages, splendid ideas and also some daring theories, which orthodoxy has rejected. These theories are called Origenism: (1) Eternal creation and the infinite number of successive worlds; (2) the pre-existence of souls (Platonist) and their fall, their taking on a body being a punishment for former sins; (3) the corporeity of angels (ethereal); (4) denial of the eternity of hell, also called universal restoration, by a general rehabilitation of the damned, including, apparently, Satan[2]; (5) denial of the resurrection of the body as contained in the Apostles' Creed; (6) the subordination of the Word to the Father; (7) and that of the Holy Spirit in relation to the Word. To Origen was attributed the doctrine that the Word acts only in rational souls, and the Spirit only in the saints. Finally, Origen was blamed, as he still is today, for his generalized allegorism in biblical teaching.

Origenist theories were the subject of lively discussions in the Church after his death. The anthropomorphites among the Egyptian monks, upset by this allegorism, were its most persistent opponents and they were supported by a noted writer, St Epiphanius, bishop of Salamis in Cyprus, who strongly denounced what he did not hesitate to call the Origenist heresy. The whole of the east was disturbed by the outbreak of fierce controversies which involved St Jerome, then in retirement in Palestine, and his friend Rufinus, a great admirer of Origen and translator of his chief work, *On First Principles*. On this occasion St Jerome fell out with Rufinus and began a dispute with him which was often accompanied by regrettable invective. It can be said that all the great doctors of the east, including Cyril, Basil and Chrysostom, were obliged to take sides for or against Origen. At the beginning of the sixth century an Origenist school was formed at the New Laura in Palestine, consisting of monks who idolized the great Alexandrine doctor. At the instigation of Ephrem, bishop of Antioch, and of Peter, bishop of Jerusalem, Justinian obtained their condemnation at a synod in 548. Origen

[2] A thesis propounded in our own times by Giovanni Papini.

and Origenism were condemned by ten detailed anathemas which Pope Vigilius confirmed. In 553, before the ecumenical council, the condemnation was repeated, this time with fifteen anathemas. It seems that Vigilius, who was present at Constantinople, once again approved them. Finally, the general council itself, without returning to the anathemas already pronounced, included Origen among the heretics. Today it is admitted that Origen did not say all that was attributed to him and that his allegorism is not in every case erroneous. What remain as Origen's are the theories about the pre-existence of souls, their fall in the body and the fact that certain stars may be animate beings.

It is less certain that he maintained the following ideas: that Christ became successively like every order of heavenly creatures, that the body of Christ was made before its union with his soul; that Christ will be crucified for the devils in another world, and that God has created everything that it was in his power to create. It is extremely doubtful that he maintained that all material creation and all bodies will end by being destroyed, that all spirits will finally be united to God like the soul of Christ, and that then the reign of Christ will come to an end.

Origen remains for us none the less an object of keen interest, combined with admiration and even veneration; for his errors, since doctrine was not yet settled, can only be regarded as material and not formal heresies. It seems certain that he was too much of a churchman not to have submitted to the decisions of the Church had these been pronounced on his theories in his own day.

MONOTHELITISM

The concessions made to the Monophysites, the condemnation of the "Three Chapters" particularly, had merely served to encourage them; they had not submitted. At the beginning of the seventh century Sergius, the Patriarch of

Constantinople, a man of clever and acute mind, conceived a new method of conciliation. There was war with the Persians. The unity of the empire was more important than ever; Sergius therefore proposed to teach that the union of the two natures in Jesus Christ was so close that in him there had never been anything but a single will and a single activity. This is what is known as Monothelitism or the theory of the one will. Meanwhile in 631 one Cyrus of Phasis became Patriarch of Alexandria which, as we know, was the capital of Monophysitism. Cyrus rallied to the teaching of Sergius. The Monophysites could exclaim triumphantly: "The Council of Chalcedon came to us and not we to it!" Some protests were, however, raised. The chief opponent of the new theory was St Sophronius, bishop of Jerusalem from 634. Sergius, in order to overcome him, sought to win over Pope Honorius by asking him to declare inopportune this distinction of one or two operations, one or two wills in Christ. Honorius, for the sake of peace, accepted his view and although at heart he approved the doctrine of Sophronius, who was orthodox, he declared for Sergius. The emperor Heraclius seized the opportunity thus offered; he published a doctrinal formulary called Ecthesis (638). This document affirmed that in Christ there was only one will, and there must be no distinction between one or two operations in him. This was heresy, for the human nature in Christ, deprived of will and of its own operation, was no longer human nature as we have it. Pope Honorius being dead, his successors Severinus, and then John IV, rejected the Ecthesis. As he was dying in 641, Heraclius declared his submission to the pope and referred the responsibility for his formulary of 638 to Sergius. But his successor Constans II (642–68) adopted it again; Rome and the west opposed it. Constans II, perturbed, replaced his Ecthesis by a new decree—the Type (648), which was limited to imposing silence on the disputed question. In 649 Pope Martin I assembled a Lateran Council at which he procured the condemnation of the Ecthesis and the Type by one hundred and five bishops. The emperor, annoyed, had the pope arrested; he was ill-treated and sent into exile, dying in Chersonese in 655. We honour him as a martyr on November 12th.

When Constans II died, his successor, Constantine IV Pogonatus (the Bearded), agreed with Pope Agatho to summon a general council at Constantinople—the sixth ecumenical council (November 2nd, 680–September 16th, 681). Monothelitism was solemnly condemned and Honorius was himself anathematized for having accepted "the impious doctrines of Sergius". But in confirming the Council Agatho's successor, Leo II, defined precisely the meaning of this condemnation, which is often cited against papal infallibility: "It is because he did not attempt to sanctify this apostolic Church with the teaching of apostolic tradition, but by profane treachery allowed its purity to be sullied." Thus he was blamed for lack of vigilance and weakness rather than for adherence to error. Today it is believed that the views of Honorius, whatever the Gallicans may have said, were always orthodox, and that he was never heretical in the proper sense of the word.

THE ICONOCLAST CONTROVERSY

We have seen that after Arianism all, or nearly all errors were connected with one another. Even Origenism, occurring before Arianism, led up to it with the theory of the subordination of the Son to the Father. With the terrible Iconoclast controversy we emerge from this circle.

In 717 an uncouth general, Leo the Isaurian, reigned as emperor in Constantinople. Of course, he understood nothing about theological matters, but he followed the custom of the empire by legislating in these affairs as in all others. Perhaps in imitation of the Caliph Jesis II, who had forbidden images in mosques, and perhaps on the advice of the Phrygian bishop, Constantine of Nacolia, in 725 he took a series of measures against the worship of images. Charles Diehl and Louis Bréhier have shown clearly that his aim was to combat the excessive influence of the monks. Edict came fast on edict, continually increasing in severity. First of all the images of saints, angels and martyrs were condemned, then images of Christ and of the Blessed Virgin were proscribed. The feelings of the faithful may be imagined, especially in the east, where basilicas were magnificently adorned with multi-coloured mosaics in honour of Christ, our Lady and the saints. Pitiless hands lent themselves to the destruction of all this artistic heritage of the past. The Patriarch of Constantinople, St Germanus, protested energetically but was deposed and replaced by Anastasius, a creature of the court. Popes Gregory II and III each in turn condemned iconoclasm, or the destruction of images, in 727 and 731. A theologian of the first rank, St John Damascene, entered the lists to defend the legitimacy of the (relative) worship paid to images, but the emperor, an extreme authoritarian, would not yield. Deplorable defections occurred among the clergy, but there was also the heroic resistance on the part of the monks and the faithful. Notable as martyrs of the persecution were some women who overturned the ladder of an iconoclast workman. The son of a successor of Leo the Isaurian, Constantine Copronymus (the Dirty), who reigned from 741 to 775, pursued the detestable policy of his father. It was only under Leo IV (775–80) and above all under Irene, Constantine's widow, that peace was restored and devotion to images re-established. Irene, in full accord with Pope Adrian I (772–95) and the Patriarch of Constantinople, St Tarasius, convoked the Council of Nicaea in 787 (the seventh ecumenical council), despite the opposition of the military party. This council clearly defined the manner in which images may legitimately be honoured. It is a relative worship, that is, one which is directed to the person represented and not to the image itself. Adrian I made great efforts to have this doctrine accepted in the west, but Charlemagne, led astray by a bad translation of the proceedings of the council, thought that it implied the honouring of images with an absolute worship. In a treatise known as the *Caroline Books*, worship of images thus misunderstood was strongly criticized, and the Council of Frankfurt condemned the practice in 794. Little by little however the misunderstanding was clarified, and the only iconoclastic crisis which was to arise in the west was due to the influence of certain Protestant sects such as the Calvinists, who even today banish images from their places of worship.

A second iconoclastic crisis broke out in the east in the ninth century under the emperors Leo the Armenian (813–20), Michael the Stammerer (820–9) and Theophilus (829–42). The first and third of these were particularly rabid. The great champion of images was then St Theodore the Studite (†826), and again it was a woman, the empress Theodora, widow of Theophilus and mother of Michael III, who had the joy of re-establishing peace by restoring the worship of images. She had scarcely come to power in 842 before she arranged with the Patriarch of Constantinople, St Methodius, to convene a council which definitely ratified the decrees of the Council of Nicaea on the subject of images.

CHAPTER V

MEDIEVAL HERESIES

GENERAL CHARACTERISTICS

It has long been customary to think of the long centuries of the Middle Ages as centuries of intellectual stagnation. The present chapter will make it clear that heresies, both individual and collective, were not lacking during that time. All these heresies showed certain common characteristics; not only were they manifestations of the extraordinary intellectual and social ferment endemic in the Middle Ages but they were also continuously recurrent protests against the feudal and clerical regime of the day. While heresies undoubtedly claim to belong solely, or chiefly, to the theological or religious sphere, in fact they also derive from anti-feudalism, anti-clericalism and the aspirations of town-dwellers towards freedom. The same social problems which confront us today already existed at that period but found expression in the theological idiom which was then current. The emancipation of the towns especially was closely associated with medieval heresies; in every case social conflicts provided a favourable climate for their development, and we should do well to bear that fact constantly in mind.

INDIVIDUAL HERESIES

Among the medieval heresies in the west we find some that were essentially individual as well as an abundance of others propagated by dissident groups; we can deal briefly with the first kind.

In the eleventh century a certain Berengarius, a former canon of Tours, then archdeacon of Angers, became the first known opponent of the real Presence in the Eucharist. According to him the consecration of bread and wine was intended to sanctify the elements by withdrawing them from common use and to give them a certain sanctifying power. For him the consecrated host was in fact only blessed bread and it was no more than a pious convention to refer to it as the body of Jesus Christ. Berengarius was immediately refuted by Adelmann of Liège, Hugh of Langres and Lanfranc of Bec, who ranked among the best theologians of the day. The doctrinal innovation was condemned at the councils of Vercelli in 1051, Paris in the same year, and Tours in 1054. In the end Berengarius retracted, but once more fell into error, again retracted and died in 1088 after a genuine conversion.

At the opposite extreme to Berengarius, who was a sort of rationalist after his own fashion, other heretics of the Middle Ages fell into false mysticism. One such was Amalric of Bena who, towards the end of the twelfth century, seems to have been inspired by the works of the philosopher, Scotus Erigena, a somewhat daring but influential Platonist. Amalric derived a kind of pantheism from his teaching, according to which God is the inmost essence of everything that exists. His followers concluded from this that everything is divine, all is good, and that there is no longer any distinction between good and evil. The Amalricians went so far as to consider themselves the instruments of the Holy Spirit; they advocated free love, became annoyed with the condemnations of the Church and ended by regarding the pope as Antichrist. Shortly after his death, between 1205 and 1207, the false teaching of Amalric was condemned by a synod of Paris in 1210, which also ordered the exhumation of his remains as being unworthy to lie in consecrated ground. Again in 1215, the Lateran Council condemned Amalrician teaching, declaring it to be ridiculous rather than heretical.

Somewhat similar ideas appeared throughout the Middle Ages, notably amongst the Beghards and the Fraticelli; the latter may well have been inspired to an even greater extent by Joachim of Flora, whose influence on most of the groups of so-called mystics of Italy and other Christian countries can be conjectured.

This Joachim, an Italian, was abbot of the Benedictine abbey of Flora in Calabria when he died on March 20th, 1202. His teaching, as astounding as his personality, can be summarized as follows: (1) Just as there are three persons in God, so there are three ages of the world, the age of the Law, the age of Christ and the age of the Holy Spirit; (2) the age of the Father or of the Law, was that of the Old Testament, a time of slavery and fear, an age of married people and of the laity; (3) the age of Christ is that of the New Testament, a mixed age of married people and of unmarried clergy living in the world; (4) the fullness of time, which would begin about the year 1260 and would be an age of monks, the time of the coming of the Holy Spirit, an age of freedom in which the everlasting Gospel would prevail. This Gospel would not be written but would be an entirely spiritual interpretation of the Old and New Testaments.

These ideas did not prevent Joachim, a gentle dreamer, from remaining a faithful son of the Church. It was only after his death that some fanatical Franciscans, headed by the famous Gerard of Borgo San Donnino, revived his writings, made them the expression of the eternal Gospel and believed themselves to be called upon to reform the Church from top to bottom. They tried to impose upon all that apostolic poverty revived so successfully by their master, St Francis of Assisi. But falling into utter rebellion, and having refused to submit to the authority of the Church, they were eventually condemned as heretics during the fourteenth century. Their movement was merely false mysticism.

THE PETROBRUSIANS

We come now to heresies taking the shape of dissident sects. First the Petrobrusians, so called from the name of their founder, Peter of Bruys, a rebellious unfrocked priest. From 1104 onwards he appears to have preached in Languedoc and Provence. He taught that infants should not be baptized because they understand nothing about it, that it is useless to pray in church because God is everywhere, that the use of the crucifix, prayers for the dead, belief in the real Presence, and, above all, obedience to the clergy should be abolished. He roused the people against the priests and monks, but a sharp reaction set in against him and one day, it was a Good Friday, while he was preparing to cook some meat on a fire of piled-up crucifixes, he was attacked by the scandalized mob and put to death (c. 1124). After him an apostate Benedictine, Henry of Lausanne, assumed the leadership of the sect; he was condemned at the Council of Pisa in 1135 and seems to have died in prison about 1145. The great adversary of this anti-clerical sect was St Bernard of Clairvaux, who often preached at the meetings where this heresy was being disseminated.

A somewhat similar sect was sponsored in the neighbourhood of Antwerp in Brabant, by an adventurer called Tanchelm of Brabant, who claimed to be the Son of God and succeeded in attracting a crowd of ignorant and fanatic followers. He was refuted by an emulator of St Bernard, the great orator St Norbert, who founded the Premonstratensians. Tanchelm died about 1115, from a blow on the head received during a voyage in a boat.

THE VAUDOIS

The foregoing petty sects were never very formidable, but this cannot be said about the Vaudois, whose founder was

Peter Valdo or Valdés, a merchant of Lyons. Anxious to live a life of perfection, Valdo steeped himself in the study of the Bible. He gave all his goods to the poor and set about preaching repentance. Disciples joined him in all good faith. At first they were called the "Poor Men of Lyons", and they considered themselves entitled to preach the Gospel to the people, but being untrained they soon alarmed the ecclesiastical authorities and the bishop of Lyons forbade them to preach. Valdo went to Rome at the time of the Lateran Council of 1179. Alexander III approved their way of life, but required them to submit to local episcopal authority regarding their preaching. The same regulations were imposed on a similar body, the Humiliati or "Poor Lombards". If the Poor Men of Lyons and the Poor Lombards had obeyed the directions given them, as St Francis of Assisi and his authentically poor men did a little later, there would have been no schism. But Valdo and his men continued to preach without permission; in vain Bishop Bellesmains called them to order, and finally Lucius III condemned them, with the Humiliati, at the Council of Verona, and in the Bull *Ad abolendam*, on November 4th, 1184. Consequently, the Vaudois separated from the Humiliati of Lombardy and set themselves up as a sect separated from the Church. They soon passed from schism to heresy, for they adopted a doctrine rather similar to that of the Donatists of the fourth century, by making the validity of the sacraments depend on the sanctity of those conferring them. But they went still further by claiming that by embracing poverty they were entitled to confer the sacraments of baptism, confirmation and the Eucharist although they had not received orders. Valdo claimed to exercise all the powers of a priest, and even of a bishop, without having been ordained or consecrated.

In order to escape the repressive measures of the ecclesiastical and civil authorities, the Vaudois established themselves in the valleys of the Cottian Alps, in Val Freissinière, Val d'Argentière, Val Louise, Val de la Dora Riparia, Val

Angrogne, while the favourite centre was the city of Pignerol and the neighbourhood of Torre Pellice. Some scattered groups however found their way to Pouille and Calabria. Much later, about 1533, the Vaudois adopted the principal teachings of the Protestant reformation, justification by faith alone, reduction of the sacraments to two only, interpretation of the Eucharist in the Calvinistic way, and the doctrine of predestination.

The Vaudois movement ended by being nothing more than an appendage of Calvinism, which brought on its adherents the sanctions of the law in the time of Francis I. By order of the parliament of Aix-en-Provence they were the victims of a shocking punitive expedition in the course of which thousands were killed. (The numbers varied between 800 and 4,000 in the twenty-two villages which were destroyed.) Enfranchised in 1848 by the Piedmontese laws of religious toleration, they considered that they had been called upon to regenerate Italy by destroying Catholicism. But their "evangelization of Italy" did not meet with the success that they had promised themselves. At present they are to be found in Piedmont, Lombardy, Venetia, Nice, Liguria, Tuscany, Rome, Southern Italy and Sicily and Rio de la Plata and neighbouring regions. But their total number does not exceed 30,000; many of them, having recovered from their prejudices against the Roman Church, cling fervently to the ecumenical movement for the reunion of the Churches.

THE ALBIGENSIANS

Much less prolonged but much more dangerous was the Albigensian heresy, which derives its name from the town of Albi, its principal centre. Its adherents are also called Cathari, from a Greek word meaning pure. The mere name suggests an oriental origin. In fact, by a process analogous to that used in paleontology for establishing the relation between fossils of different periods, it would seem possible to connect

the heresy of the Cathari of France and Italy with Manicheism, by way of the Bogomili of Bulgaria in the ninth century
and the Paulicians of Asia in the seventh century. Consequently, this is the place to speak of that Manicheism to which
Augustine remained more or less attached for nine of his
early years.

Manicheism derives its name from its founder, Mani, a
native of Babylonia, who was connected through his father
Patek with the royal family of Arsacides in Persia. Mani was
born on April 14th, 216; his father is thought to have belonged
to an Encratite sect whose members even then called themselves "the pure" and wore white clothing. It is not improb-
able that Mani had been brought up from his earliest youth
in a tradition of anxious pursuit of purity, by the avoidance
of matter which was held to be the source of all evil and
impurity. But at a very early date Mani felt called to a
prophetic mission and his teaching rests on a conception of
uninterrupted divine prophecy. He identifies himself, therefore, with the Paraclete which sets him in a Christian atmos-
phere but outside orthodox Christianity. He took his teaching
from four different sources: the old naturist religion of Baby-
lon, Parseeism or the religion of Zoroaster, Buddhism for
morals and asceticism, and Christianity for prophecy and the
theory of salvation, but this Christianity is fed by the apocryphal rather than by the authentic Gospels. In short, Mani
is a sort of Mohammed before his time, a Mohammed who
did not succeed.

His system is founded on dualism, a twofold eternal principle, of good and of evil. The struggle arises between primitive man, whom God had created good, and Satan the prince
of darkness. Man bears traces of his defection and woman
still more. The dualism in us consists in the conflict between
the spirit and the flesh. Jesus took on an apparent body
(Docetism) in order to save man. Salvation consists in freeing
the particles of light in us which have been lost in the darkness of the body. Not all reach this state of freedom to the

same degree. The perfect disciples of Mani are those who observe the three seals: the seal of the mouth (perpetual abstinence from wine, meat and all impure conversation), the seal of the hand (avoidance of all servile work), and the seal of the belly (absolute continence). Those who practise this ideal are the elect; lesser disciples are called hearers. In his youth Augustine was one of these but went no further.

We find similar ideas amongst the Spanish Priscillianists of the fifth and sixth centuries, and amongst the various groups we have already mentioned. In France, Catharism shows itself in the twelfth century in Champagne, Languedoc and Provence. The name of Albigensians was soon given almost everywhere to groups of them far removed from Albi. The Manicheism from which they derived is clearly to be discerned among these heretics. As they developed Manicheism was however affected by new elements, anti-clericalism, anarchism, anti-militarism and communism. The distinction between the elect or perfect and the simple hearers or believers remained the basis of the organization of the sect. The elect practised a rigorous asceticism which made a deep impression on the common people. A noble lady of Languedoc used to tell how she went to visit one of these perfect: "He struck me as very strange," she said. "For a very long time he sat on a chair, motionless as a tree-trunk and oblivious of everything going on around him." Today we should compare him to an Indian fakir. The perfect had a horror of marriage, since it perpetuates this satanic illusion of life on earth; they thus practised absolute continence and discouraged the believers from marrying. They also condemned the taking of oaths and military service, and considered voluntary suicide as the ideal of sanctity. Some of them opened their veins to die in a bath, or took poison. But the most widespread form of suicide consisted in undergoing the *endura*, or allowing themselves to starve to death. In order to enter a state of perfection the elect received a kind of spiritual baptism called *consolamentum*, entirely spiritual because water was accursed, like all matter. The believers had no other obligation than to adore the elect and to feed them; provided this were done they were able to live as they liked. However, they also received the *consolamentum*, but on their deathbed, when no further chance of recovery remained; to avoid all chance of a return to health, they were compelled, or they voluntarily undertook, to undergo the *endura*, going on hunger strike so as not to lose the fruits of their regeneration.

Such a doctrine was so clearly opposed to the Christian religion and to the whole of a society founded on that religion, and indeed even to the civilization which Christianity had brought into being, that it is not surprising that fierce opposition to it was aroused. On the Catholic side this opposition was at first conducted with true apostolic zeal and charity. St Bernard preached repeatedly against the Cathari. Fifty years later, Innocent III was startled by the progress of the heresy and urged the prelates and noblemen of the south of France to unite their efforts to fight it. He sent legates to direct the evangelization of the contaminated districts, but he solemnly ordered the use of pacific means. "We command you", he wrote to his legates on November 19th, 1206, "to choose men of proved virtue. . . . Modelling themselves on the poverty of Christ, and poorly clad, they are to seek out the heretics and try, with God's grace, to snatch them from error." Among the most fervent of these Catholic apostles we find, in 1206, a Spanish bishop, Diego de Azevedo, and one of his canons of Osma, Dominic Guzman, who later founded the great Order of Friars Preachers or Dominicans, the better to combat the heresy.

Unhappily, violence soon made its appearance. On January 15th, 1208, the papal legate, Peter of Castelnau, was assassinated by fanatics. Innocent III then called Christian noblemen to a crusade against the rebels. But it was easier to throw these rough feudal warriors into the fray than to keep them within the bounds of Christian moderation. Deplorable excesses occurred on both sides. The crusade was directed by Count Simon de Montfort. Unconscious animosities between the lords of the north and the south accounted for much. The crusaders were intent on one thing only, to dispossess the heretics of their belongings in order to enrich themselves. The capture of Béziers was accompanied by bloody butchery. The battle of Muraille on September 12th, 1213, was decisive. In the end, it was the French royal house which succeeded in reaping the benefit of the disruption of feudal ownership caused by the terrible Albigensian war. The lamentable events of this war must largely be associated with the increase of repressive measures against heresy by the court of the Inquisition, created in 1184 at the Council of Verona; this was first entrusted to the bishops until about 1233, when it passed to the delegates of the Holy See who were very frequently Dominicans. From 1224 the civil law prescribed the death penalty for obstinate heretics.

WYCLIF'S HERESY

The heresies of the Vaudois and the Cathari might be regarded as anarchic attempts to reform the Church which was sullied by too many abuses. This same characteristic appears in Wyclif and John Huss, before being further developed by Luther and the innovators of the sixteenth century. But instead of obscure movements arising among the people it is now university trained men who try to undertake the reshaping of dogma and the repression of moral disorders within the Church.

Wyclif was essentially an Oxford man. Born in Yorkshire, between 1324 and 1328, he went to Oxford in 1345, where the black death interrupted his studies between 1349 and 1353. Then he became Master of Balliol College and vicar of Fillingham. He took his doctorate in theology in 1372. He enjoyed the plurality of benefices which was one of the regrettable evils of the times. From 1374 onwards he wrote a whole series of works which earned him the favours of the Crown; from that time he was the advocate of the rights of the state against the papacy. His chief works are: "Of the Divine Dominion" (1375), "Of the Civil Dominion" (1375), "Of the Faith of Scripture" (1378), "Of the Church" (1378) —largely used by John Huss a little later—"Of Christian Order" (1379), "Of Apostasy" (1379), "Of the Eucharist" (1379), "Trialogus" (autumn 1382), this being the most important of all his works. All of these and several other less important works were of course written in Latin. But he also published some "reformist tracts" in English and popularized an English translation of the Bible. He organized popular preachers and under the name of "poor priests" sent them about the country; soon these came to be nicknamed Lollards by the public, a name which seems to mean "mumblers". In February, 1377, he was prosecuted by Bishop William de Courtenay but the court defended him. On the other hand Gregory X condemned him and cited him to appear to answer the charge of heresy; he protested against this citation in the name of English freedom and dubbed the pope Antichrist. Thenceforth the name of Wyclif was to the fore in all social agitations, and the peasants quoted his authority against exactions of which they were the victims. Bishop William de Courtenay again took the matter in hand, this time with the support of the court. The synod of Blackfriars, May 17th–21st, 1382, condemned all Wyclif's teachings and purged Oxford University of his followers. He withdrew to his parish at Lutterworth, south of Leicester, and continued to write voluminously until he died on December 31st, 1384. He was given a religious funeral for he had never been formally excommunicated, but after the Council of Constance had condemned his teaching on May 4th, 1415, the Bishop of Lincoln, the diocesan of Lutterworth, received an order to exhume his remains, to have them burned and the ashes thrown into the river; this was not done until 1428.

Wyclif's teaching is condensed in the forty-five propositions extracted from his writings and condemned at the Council of Constance and by two Bulls of Martin V in 1418. His system is a kind of fatalistic pantheism, according to which God is everything and everything is God. All that happens is of necessity; God predestines some souls to heaven, others to hell. The Church is no more than the invisible society of the predestinated. There is no divine authority other than the Bible. The Roman Church is the synagogue of Satan. The religious orders are diabolical institutions, and the dogma of transubstantiation is heresy. Christ is indeed present in the Eucharist, but at the same time as the bread and the wine, which are not destroyed.

One of Wyclif's most anti-social theories was that of sovereignty, or the divine and civil dominions, which was the title of one of his first works. According to this only God is sovereign; he alone has dominion over all things. The king possesses his state only under the authority of God and he can only exercise his power if he has subjected himself to God, that is, if he is in a state of grace. Man in a state of mortal sin can exercise neither sovereignty nor rights of ownership. On the other hand, man in a state of grace is really sovereign of the whole universe, in God. The papacy possesses no power whatever, either direct or indirect, in the civil sphere. However, as only God knows those who are in a state of grace, Wyclif found himself obliged to deny all practical efficacy to the revolutionary ideas which he held in theory. None the less they contained explosive matter, and this explains the great rise of the Lollards who were harshly suppressed by Henry IV of Lancaster after 1400; they were hunted down mercilessly and finally disappeared entirely.

JOHN HUSS AND THE HUSSITES

There is a close connection between the heresy of John Huss and that of Wyclif. Huss was born about 1369 at

Husinecz, of a peasant family. He studied at Prague, became a preacher at the Bethlehem chapel in Prague which he turned into a centre of ecclesiastical reform as well as of Czech patriotism.

John Huss was an ascetic. His burning eloquence, exemplary life and pale austere countenance all evoked the enthusiasm of his hearers; his popularity was further enhanced by his hatred of foreigners, his reforming zeal and studious devotion to the Gospel. One of his latest biographers, Ernest Denis, speaks of his "inflexible humility", a humility which perhaps hid an overweening pride. A conscious zeal for reform took the place of theology, philosophy and orthodoxy. He was by no means an original thinker, but at that moment the teachings of Wyclif, imported from Oxford, owing to the interchange of Czech students, were the subject of lively discussions in Prague. One of the most ardent Bohemian Wyclifites was a young student called Jerome of Prague; Huss also threw himself into these discussions. Like Wyclif he conceded that the Scriptures are the only source of all divine truth, that Christ is the only head of the Church, that the papacy is no more than a *de facto* institution in which Christ had no part, that every superior who fell into mortal sin lost his authority, that the Church is composed only of the predestined and that predestination is infallible. A number of these ideas were to recur with Luther, but he was by no means influenced by Huss in the religious revolution which he instigated a century later.

A racial conflict was added to the religious controversies aroused by the preaching of Huss. He prevailed upon King Wenceslas to concede that the body of Czech members should have three votes in the University of Prague while the three other nations, Bavaria, Saxony and Poland, should have only one. At once, it is said, 2,000 students and teachers left Prague and went off to found the University of Leipzig (1409). But John Huss, victorious on this point, was opposed by his bishop on account of his Wyclifite teaching. In the summer of 1412 a papal Bull excommunicated him and placed the chapel where he preached under an interdict. Huss appealed on the one hand to Christ, but like Luther a century later, he also appealed to the nobility and to the people. Believing that Scripture supported him he was able to shelter his "inflexible humility" beneath awareness of his biblical infallibility. All the leading heretics acted thus, and they continue to do so. In these circumstances it was inconsistent of him to appear before the Council of Constance. Possibly he hoped to convince the Council. Armed with a safe-conduct from the emperor Sigismund, he appeared there on November 28th, 1414. He declared that he was ready to die rather than to admit that he was in error, and we may believe that he was sincere in this. The examination of his teaching led directly to that of Wyclif which he had copied sometimes word for word. Now, as we have seen, the forty-five propositions of Wyclif were condemned on May 4th, 1415, as being notoriously heretical, or erroneous, seditious and finally scandalous. The discussions were directed by a French prelate, Peter d'Ailly. Huss tried to put on a bold front and defend Wyclif's ideas which he had made his own, but he was greatly mistaken if he thought that the fluency and heat of his words could take the place of orthodoxy for such judges. Eventually he confined himself to appealing to Christ.

All hope of making him yield had to be abandoned. His writings were condemned to the flames on June 24th, 1415. On July 6th he was given a final warning, but not a word of retractation could be obtained from him, and sentence was pronounced upon him: "The holy Council has proof that John remains stubborn and incorrigible . . . the assembly therefore decrees that the accused shall be deposed and degraded, and that after he has been cast out of the Church he shall be delivered to the secular arm."

And so it was done. On the same day the unfortunate John Huss was delivered to the flames without having agreed to abjure. The emperor Sigismund has been accused of violating the safe-conduct by this action, but this is open to dispute, for the safe-conduct was not intended to remove him from the legal justice of the time but to protect him while he was travelling. His friend Jerome of Prague was accused in his turn; he fled but was recaptured, consented to submit but then withdrew his abjuration; he was executed as a relapsed heretic on May 30th, 1416.

CHAPTER VI

THE PROTESTANT

REVOLUTION

A CALAMITY

There are two singularly deplorable dates in the long history of the Church. The first is that on which the schism broke out between the Greek Church and the Latin Church on July 16th, 1054, through the excommunication imposed upon Michael Cerularius, Patriarch of Constantinople. The second is October 31st, 1517, when the Protestant revolution began and the "Theses on Indulgences" were nailed to the church door by Martin Luther, the Augustinian friar.

The Greek schism cannot properly be called a heresy, for which reason we have not described it in this short historical summary. There were precedents for it: the schism of Acacius which we have noted, and the schism of Photius in the ninth century. Reunion was twice effected, at the Council of Lyons in 1274 and at the Council of Florence in 1438–9, but both these reconciliations were ephemeral. There is however little which separates us from the Greek Church as a whole, which calls itself (and indeed we call it) the Orthodox Church in order to recognize the authenticity of its faith in general. And when we pray most fervently for reunion it is primarily for a reconciliation between the two sister Churches, the Roman Church, mother and centre of the Churches, and the Orthodox Church.

The Protestant revolution was unfortunately a much more

serious matter which explains why, in speaking of it, we use the term "calamity". In the triple unity desired by Christ for his Church, unity of faith, unity of communion, and unity of government, only the last is affected by a schism. But in· the Protestant revolution all three forms of unity were affected and unity has been broken without repair, and in the accepted phrase "the seamless robe of Christ has been torn".

THE CAUSES OF PROTESTANTISM

In studying the causes of Protestantism it is usual to draw a sombre picture of abuses which sullied the Church: worldliness of the papacy and of a great proportion of the clergy from top to bottom of the scale, the invasion of paganism under cover of a return to classical Greek and Roman antiquity in humanism, the development of nationalism and a policy called realistic, that is, one which disregards all moral law in order to envisage results only, a policy of which Machiavelli became the historian and admiring theorist. All that is true, but it is not the essential. Disorder and uneasiness within the Church there might be, heresy might appear, but it was certainly not inevitable that it should take the form of separated Churches and degenerate into numerous schisms that have so far proved incurable. The most serious in this unhappy revolution within the Church was that which tried to effect a reform of dogma, to return to the "purity" of Christianity, in short to monopolize the great name of reform which had been current throughout the Church for centuries. Reform the Church indeed! What a grandiose and alluring proposition! But three mistakes were to be avoided: (1) a belief that the Church, having fallen short of her primitive ideals, could as a Church err in matters of faith; (2) to imagine that the pure faith, lost to the Church, could be rediscovered as classical antiquity is rediscovered in a Greek or Latin manuscript; (3) to think that once Christian doctrine has been rediscovered by the efforts of one or of several reformers, it could always be preserved from any further alteration.

There was error concerning the past, for the Church, even if corrupted by abuses, had her Founder's promise of the assistance of the Holy Spirit that she could not be false to the deposit of the true faith. There was error concerning the present, for no human power whatever could rediscover the faith by mere recourse to the Scriptures, that is, by exegesis and philology. And there was error concerning the future, in the sense that this recourse to Scripture, turned into an absolute principle of reform, was, on the contrary, to stand revealed as one of dispersion and endless redivision for those very people who placed all their confidence in it. Having noted this, we may now summarize the essential facts.

LUTHER AND THE BREACH OF UNITY

Martin Luther was born on November 10th, 1483, at Eisleben in Saxony. His father was a miner whose only bequest to his son was, in Luther's own words, a "rough Saxon temperament". His mother, Margaret Ziegler, a firm believer, was very superstitious and had a taste for stories of the devil and sorcery.

Young Luther's schooldays were made up of suffering and privations, despite which he did well at his studies, which meant a course in the decayed and arid scholasticism of the times. He graduated as a master of arts in 1505 at the university of Erfurt. His father, proud of his son's success, thought of making him a lawyer, for this was the best career in which to make a fortune, and he was consequently very disappointed when he found that his son had entered the Augustinian monastery of Erfurt on July 17th, 1505, without his permission. What had happened? Young Luther, returning to his homeland, had been overtaken at the gates of Erfurt by a fierce storm, on July 2nd, 1505. He imagined himself at death's door. Distracted with fear, impetuously he vowed to enter the religious life if he escaped from the lightning. A fortnight later he kept his vow, but this wholly immature vocation was to be a burden upon his whole existence. At first all went well; he underwent his novitiate and took his vows. On May 2nd, 1507, he was ordained priest, and in the following year he went from Erfurt to Wittenberg as a professor of the new university in that city. He journeyed to Rome in 1510–11 on business for his monastery, but this in no way affected his faith in the papacy, despite his later assertions. On his return, however, he became an opponent of the party of strict observance in his Order, making a point of obedience to his superiors in faith and humility. He was already showing signs of defiance towards what he later called "righteousness by works", or "personal righteousness". But he pursued his studies and received the doctorate of theology in 1512. Like so many of his generation he was disgusted with scholasticism[1]; he showed a preference for biblical study, but not without the personal conviction that he was reverting to a field that had been abandoned. He was unaware, at least to begin with, that together with him in this biblical movement were such men as John Colet in Oxford, Lefèvre of Étaples in Paris and Erasmus in various cities. First he commented on the Psalms in 1514, and a year later he turned to the Epistle to the Romans wherein he made, or thought he had made, important discoveries for the reform of Christian dogma. We who can read the whole story are certain that he only read St Paul in the light of the secret and unconscious demands of his own enthusiastic temperament, which was given to extremes, and was moreover devoured by scruples and torments that nothing could soothe.

Today we call this subjective exegesis, that is, adapting texts to fit personal experience. In his case this experience showed him that sin cannot be conquered in us, that it is inherent in our nature, and that salvation would be impossible if it consisted in purification from all sin. He had reached the

[1] This scholasticism was in fact thoroughly decadent, and Luther was unconsciously affected by the pernicious influence of Nominalism.

point where he confused feeling with consent, of being no longer able to distinguish between concupiscence and sin, of regarding man and all creation under the dominion of an implacable fatalism. And he thought that he found in St Paul both a striking description of his own interior state and the certain remedy for all his own anguish. Proud of his discovery, he purposed to spread it throughout the entire Church, making it into a principle of liberation, reform and universal salvation. Yet he does not seem to have envisaged a breach with the Church; it occurred without his being aware of it. Once in possession of his doctrine, however, and in spite of a certain wavering and modification of a more or less conscious and voluntary nature, he would no longer depart from it.

The occasion—and it was only the occasion—of the breach was the question of indulgences. A deplorable traffic, which today we rightly condemn, at that time had gradually insinuated itself into Church practice and for motives which were sometimes almost praiseworthy. On this occasion it was a question of raising funds for St Peter's basilica in Rome. A murmuring discontent was rife in Germany, and even in the taverns Roman greed was being criticized. Luther had already attacked the doctrine of indulgences, and he hastily drew up ninety-five theses which he nailed to the doors of the collegiate church in Wittenberg.

Among these theses was the following: "The treasures of indulgences are the nets with which men's riches are now fished. If the pope knew the exactions made by the preachers of indulgences he would prefer the basilica of St Peter to be reduced to ashes, rather than to have it built with the skin, flesh and bones of his sheep."

This produced a tremendous impression. Nobody came forward to dispute Luther's theses, but a written controversy began between him and the Roman theologians. With his Saxon crudeness, Luther first upset the theologians and then offended the papal legate, Cardinal Cajetan of Augsburg, and being unable to yield to the latter's representations nor to reach any agreement with him, he appealed to the "better-informed pope" on October 22nd, 1518, and then to the pope in a general council on November 28th, 1518.

Immediately, however, indulgences fell into second place; the main theme was now the dogma, so dear to Luther, of the certainty of salvation through faith alone without works. It is strange that after he had challenged the doctrine and practice of indulgences on the ground that they bred a feeling of security he should now make security by faith the central dogma of his teaching.

The Disputation of Leipzig (June 27th–July 16th, 1519), instead of settling these matters, made them infinitely worse. The Catholic theologian, John Eck, confronted him with the definitions of the councils, particularly that of Constance, against John Huss. Rather than give way, Luther rejected the authority of councils, relying on Scripture alone; after this there could be no further doubt about his condemnation by Rome. At this crucial moment of his evolution he was encouraged by revolutionary humanists, like Ulrich von Hutten and some German knights, hostile to Rome. With this support he decided on a breach. This took place in his view on July 10th, 1520, for on that date he wrote: "The die is cast! I scorn the fury and the favour of Rome; I no longer wish for reconciliation nor communion with them for all eternity!" And on July 17th, in a second letter, he explains: "Silvester von Schaumberg and Franz von Sickingen (two German revolutionary knights) have freed me henceforth from all human fear."

In point of fact he was to find a far more effective ally in his own sovereign, the Elector of Saxony, of whose secret dispositions he was unaware.

FORMATION OF THE PROTESTANT CHURCH

After 1520 events moved quickly. On August 1st Luther published his manifesto "To the Christian Nobility of Germany for the Reform of the Christian State". In this he said that all Christians are equal (universal priesthood), that all have equally the right of recourse to the Bible, the interpretation of which is in no way reserved to the Church (integral biblicism), and that the emperor and princes have more right than the pope to summon a general council (Caesaro-papalism). In the following October he published his second great reforming work, "Prelude on the Babylonian Captivity of the Church"; in this he devoted himself to the doctrine of the sacraments, which he reduced to two, baptism and the Eucharist—or three at most, by including penance. Finally, in November, he published his little book on the freedom of the Christian man, which is one of the best expositions of his teaching.

This teaching is as follows: (1) Man has been totally corrupted by original sin and everything he does is mortal sin. Salvation by works is impossible. (2) God doubtless imposes his Law on us in the Old Testament, but this is unfeasible; its only aim is to discourage us, to make us despair, to throw us into the arms of mercy. (3) When the Law has brought us to despair, faith suddenly causes to shine before our eyes the brightness of salvation, through the merits of Jesus Christ, who died for us on the cross. (4) God has predestined some from all eternity to hell, those to whom he denies faith, and others to heaven, those to whom he grants it. (5) The sacraments of baptism and the Eucharist have no other efficacy than to arouse faith in our hearts.

But Rome had spoken. The Bull *Exsurge Domine*, of June 15th, 1520, condemned forty-one propositions taken from Luther's works. By way of reply he publicly burnt the Bull at Wittenberg on December 10th in the presence of the university students. On January 3rd, 1521, he was excommunicated. The emperor summoned him to the Diet of Worms to demand a recantation of his errors. This emperor was the youthful Charles of Hapsburg, known as Charles the Fifth. Luther, at his second appearance, on April 18th, 1521, made the following famous declaration to the Diet: "Unless I am convinced by scriptural proofs and by evident reasons I am bound by the texts which I have quoted, and my conscience is bound by the word of God, for I believe neither in the pope nor in councils alone which are assuredly often mistaken and disproved. I neither can, nor will recant anything, for it is neither safe nor right to act against one's conscience. God help me, Amen." That was the consummation of the schism.

Immediately after his refusal to recant Luther was banished from the empire, but as he was protected by a safe-conduct, he set out on his return journey. On the way he was seized by certain knights, acting on secret orders from his sovereign, the Elector of Saxony, and taken to the castle of Wartburg, above Eisenach, where he was to remain for ten months disguised as a knight. In his absence his friends at Wittenberg carried on the movement and very soon went far beyond anything that he had anticipated or planned. Canon Karlstadt and a monk, Zwilling, took charge of the revolution, to the great alarm of Melanchthon, who was less audacious. They advocated marriage of priests, suppression of monastic vows, the throwing open of convents and the abolition of the Mass. From a distance Luther burned with impatience; he approved somewhat regretfully and at the same time deplored their restiveness. One day certain "prophets" came to Wittenberg saying that they were inspired by the Holy Spirit, and proclaiming that adults must be re-baptized because, they said, infant baptism was invalid. At last Luther could contain himself no longer; boldly, and in violation of the sentence of banishment from the empire, he left his retreat and returned to Wittenberg, relying on the protection of his sovereign. For eight days in succession he preached, trying to restore order, but principally to retrieve his own authority. He strongly condemned the extremists whom he termed fanatics, silenced his imitators, Karlstadt and Münzer, chief of the re-baptizers or Anabaptists. But instead of returning to the Roman Church, which in his view was the seat of Antichrist (the pope), he organized a regional Church which he eventually placed under the full authority of the sovereign. Having dreamed of a free Church, he arrived by a curious contradiction, at a state Church.[2]

He now faced two ways; he wanted a Church which was ordered, regulated and policed, in which everybody, pastors and faithful, obeyed implicitly, but this Church remained hostile to Rome, and thus was hostile to all change except its own. He became extremely conservative, according to his own interpretation of the term, and declined all compromise. When in 1525 the "Peasants" rose in the name of the Gospel, he approved their bloody repression by the nobility: "Good Lords," he wrote, "deliver us, help us, pity us, poor men that we are; cut down, smite, butcher as many as you can. . . . An anarchist is not worthy of being answered with reasons for he will not accept them. One must reply to such men with the fist!" And when his friends protested against such ruthlessness he replied even more harshly: "The ass wants to receive blows and the people want to be ruled by force. God knew that well, for he did not give governments a fox's brush but a sword!"

About the same time Luther broke his monastic vows, on June 13th, 1525, by taking a wife, a former nun, Catherine von Bora, who bore him five children, three boys and two girls.

Imitating Saxony, other princely states embraced the so-called Lutheran Reform. Whole countries fell away from the Catholic Church, Hesse, many towns in the empire, Sweden,

[2]After criticizing Rome in the name of the Gospel, Luther then founded an orthodoxy guaranteed by the state.

Denmark, Norway, and, by means of secularization, some ecclesiastical states, as well as the duchy of Prussia in Poland. The growing force of the Lutheran schism could be seen when in 1529 at the Diet of Spires five princes and fourteen towns of the empire protested against the decisions of the Catholic majority. Thenceforth the dissidents received the name of Protestants.

When Luther died on February 18th, 1546, his "Church" was strongly established and had taken its place on the political chessboard of Europe. But although they had shattered Christian unity the Protestants were unable to maintain unity among themselves. Other churches were formed, often as hostile to each other as they were towards the Catholic Church.

Before we leave Luther we may note his chief works after the breach; in 1525 appeared *De Servo Arbitrio*—"Of Slave-Will", written to refute Erasmus who had defended the existence of free-will, without which no morality is conceivable and therefore no authentic religion; in 1529 came the Little, followed by the Great Catechism; in 1537 the Articles of Smalkald, a complete exposition of Lutheran teaching; and finally in 1545 a furious work, "Against the Papacy founded at Rome by the devil", provoked by the meeting of the Council of Trent.

Luther was a man of passionate feeling and possessed an ardent and impetuous heart, together with a fertile mind lacking the faculty of clear thought and served by an astounding assurance; his was a popular and captivating eloquence, though often trivial; by temperament he was violent, incapable of restraint, poise or loyalty towards an adversary, and yet a lover of material order, of civil and religious discipline. Added to this, he had a vivid imagination haunted by strange visions and irresistible obsessions; he has sometimes been called the *doctor hyperbolicus*—"the excessive doctor".

ZWINGLI AND ZWINGLIANISM

Simultaneously with Luther's revolt against the authority of Rome, which had been considerably assisted by regional reaction against the emperor's authority, a movement began in Zürich in Switzerland though under a slightly different form. At its head was Ulrich Zwingli, a parish priest of the city. He was born in Wildhaus on January 1st, 1484, fifty days after Luther. After a successful education at Berne, Basle and Vienna, though with a more humanistic bias than Luther's, he became parish priest of Glarus, a military chaplain in Italy with Swiss troops, and finally parish priest at Einsiedeln. Unlike Luther, he had a lively admiration for Erasmus and very soon acquired the habit of reading the New Testament in Greek, for which Luther reproached him as a sign of pride. He remained firmly attached to the pope and to Rome, but his private life was far from edifying. When, after his breach with the Church, he was officially married, he merely regularized in his own fashion his former liaison with a widow named Anna Reinhard who gave him a son after four months of marriage.

He had become parish priest of the principal church in Zürich in 1519. At this time Luther's ideas were beginning to be widely noised abroad. Zwingli always denied that he was a disciple of Luther, but there is no doubt that he desired to emulate him and to follow his pattern. From 1519 to 1520, like Luther, he came out boldly against indulgences, and in 1522 against the Lenten fast, against ecclesiastical celibacy which he had never managed to practise properly, against the authority of councils and of the pope. He had the advantage of the energetic support of the Zürich city council; soon he adopted radical measures, the expulsion of monks, destruction of images (1524), abolition of the Mass (1525), and the obligation for the citizens of Zürich to attend Zwinglian meetings on pain of legal penalties. Just like Luther, Zwingli had evolved from a free Church to an authoritarian Church controlled by the republican government of the city, while Luther had placed his under the control of his sovereign. Moreover, in his sphere, Zwingli proved as intolerant as Luther had done in his, by violently persecuting the Anabaptists in 1527.

However, the biblical principles which Zwingli adopted, again like Luther, led him to quite different conclusions regarding the Eucharist. A violent quarrel broke out between the two leaders of the new reform in 1525, and this conflict is still maintained. While Luther, completely rejecting the Catholic dogma of transubstantiation, retained the real Presence under the form of consubstantiation, as Wyclif had done in England, Zwingli categorically rejected any mode of presence. He translated Christ's words "This is my body" by "This represents my body". Karlstadt had already given these same words quite another interpretation. Another reformer, Ecolampadius, who dominated Basle, sided with Zwingli by translating the words as "This is the image of my body". Biblicism gave birth to diversity, and this was the most serious of the "variations" in Protestantism and one which is just as acute today. Vainly the Lutheran Prince Philip of Hesse, who treated the matter as a policial one, tried to achieve unity on this critical point in his Marburg Colloquy in 1529, but be found it impossible to eliminate the differences between the Zwinglians and the Lutherans.

Zwingli had succeeded in creating a dissident Church, quite different from that of Wittenberg, not only in Zürich but also in several Swiss cantons and in a number of cities in the empire. Strasbourg held an intermediate position between Lutheranism and Zwinglianism, under the leadership of Bucer and Capito. But Zwingli, imprudent enough to put himself at the head of the Zürich troops in a war against the Catholic cantons of the neighbourhood, was vanquished and killed at the battle of Cappel on October 11th, 1531. His place at Zürich was taken by Bullinger, a man of much calmer character. Zwinglianism persisted, but at length merged with Calvinism, which must now be mentioned.

JOHN CALVIN AND CALVINISM

Luther, Zwingli and Calvin are the three important names of the Protestant revolution. Calvin, who was the youngest of the three, was also by far the most systematic, the most vigorously logical and intransigent, as well as the most energetic organizer.

John Calvin was born at Noyon in Picardy on July 10th, 1509. At an early age he inherited a small benefice the revenues of which helped him to complete his studies. In August, 1523, he came to Paris and shortly afterwards entered the college of Montaigu, to which shortly afterwards came Ignatius of Loyola, founder of the Jesuits. Calvin was then a studious young man, strict, a little shy and, so it is said, nicknamed "the accusative" by his companions.

France was far from having escaped the reformation controversies. One of the most eminent professors of the University of Paris, Lefèvre of Étaples, a man of piety and learning, had advocated the return to biblical studies, but in an entirely orthodox manner. The Bishop of Meaux, William Briçonnet, becoming his disciple, had formed a reformist circle known as the Meaux Group, but the Sorbonne, which had adopted a strong position against Luther and condemned over a hundred propositions taken from his works, took exception to what was happening at Meaux and the group was soon obliged to break up (1524), some reverting to integral Catholicism, others retaining a moderate reformist position and others again eagerly joining the revolutionary camp. Among the last the most turbulent was William Farel, who soon went to Switzerland, where we shall shortly encounter him. In Paris itself opposition to the heresy showed itself by executions, the most resounding of which was that of the knight, Louis de Berquin, in 1529. One can be sure that in the student world events were passionately discussed and from many differing viewpoints. For long Calvin resisted the reformist temptation. He intended to study law rather than the Bible, and showed signs of humanist leanings. However, his attention was turned towards the Bible first by his cousin Peter Robert Olivétan, in 1528, then by a Lutheran professor of Greek, Melchior Wolmar, who taught at Bourges. He also seems to have been embittered by the dispute in which his father, Gerard Calvin, became involved with the chapter of Noyon and which caused him to be excommunicated. After his father died in 1531, Calvin abandoned the law in favour of humanist classical studies, and it was only in the beginning of 1533 that he allied himself with a reformist group in Paris with clearly Lutheran tendencies. He was immediately noticed for his vigorous mind and the elegance of his style. At this time he became enamoured of Luther's theology which taught him to be introspective, to experience a horror of sin, to despair of his salvation, and to cast himself upon faith in Christ to find consolation. It can be said that one of the most powerful attractions of Lutheran teaching was this kind of romantic mysticism of consolation made fashionable by the monk of Wittenberg. For his friend Nicolas Cop, who was elected rector of the University, Calvin composed a sermon which was preached on All Saints' Day in 1533; it was so full of Lutheran ideas that it created a scandal. Nicolas Cop, who had preached it, had to flee, and Calvin, its author, felt it wise to imitate him. This episode decided his future; he gave up his ecclesiastical benefices on May 4th, 1534, and left France towards the end of the same year. Having taken refuge in Basle, he composed in Latin his famous treatise "On the Institution of the Christian Religion", which he never ceased to emend and improve and which subsequently became the theological manual of his Church in its French translation of 1559. But it still remained for the young Calvin to find a field of activity; this was assured to him quite unexpectedly by William Farel who, as we have seen, was one of the Meaux group. Calvin went from Basle to Ferrara to put himself under the protection of the French princess Renée de Ferrara, but being unable to remain was making his way back to Basle or Strasbourg to settle there, when by chance he came to Geneva. Farel, who knew his worth, had word of his arrival. He sought him out and in a moving and solemn entreaty called on him to stay there to help with the reformation. Calvin remained. In the month of August, 1536, he set to work, but he was much more absolute than Luther or Zwingli. Each in his own way had subjected the Church to the State, while naturally keeping the theological direction on account of their biblical knowledge. Calvin, always in the name of the Bible, resolved to subject the State to the Church. He immediately posed as God's representative. The citizens of Geneva were threatened with the prospect of being under the yoke of a theocracy which was only a Bibliocracy dominated by Calvin. He was faced with some opposition. In 1538 Calvin and Farel were driven out for the first time. Calvin withdrew to Strasbourg, where he married a widow named Idelette de Bure, by whom he had an only son who died in infancy. But in Geneva his followers regained the upper hand; he was recalled to that city, and after clearly stating his conditions, returned on September 13th, 1541, an absolute victor. It can be said that he "reigned" uninterruptedly until his death in 1564. Two things about Lutheranism had struck him: the reproach of immorality made against Lutherans on account of their principle of the uselessness of works and of salvation by faith alone, and the reproach of doctrinal indiscipline.

As soon as he was master of Geneva he concerned himself with preventing such reproaches. He achieved this by the extraordinary feat of maintaining the principle of the uselessness of works, and of salvation by faith alone, and at the same time asserting loudly the necessity of works as a sign of faith. His teaching on this point gave birth to a rigorous morality which has been dubbed Puritanism. It might be said that this rigorism took the place of the mysticism of consolation imbibed from Luther which had at first attracted him. In Calvinism consolation does not reside, as with Luther, in the certitude of salvation through faith in Jesus Christ, but in the prodigious consciousness of divine election made perceptible by the purity of personal virtue. There we have one of the essential distinctions between Calvinism and Lutheranism.

The use of excommunication is another way in which Calvin's forcefulness is manifested no less surprisingly. Luther had maintained the dogma of a real presence but in fact had not contrived to make any use of excommunication. Calvin on the other hand succeeded by another *tour de force* in depriving the sacrament of the Eucharist of the real Presence, denying both transubstantiation and consubstantiation, thus making the Eucharist a mere symbol and yet at the same time made excommunication from this symbol so formidable a matter that the very highest in the city of Geneva trembled when he threatened such a censure.

He caused the council to adopt the Ecclesiastical Ordinances which governed the whole organization of his Church. These distinguished four types of office: pastors, doctors, elders and deacons. The general direction of the Calvinist Church was entrusted to a consistory composed of six pastors and twelve elders who supervised the discipline of the faithful. It was required to meet every week, to summon before it those delinquents who had been denounced by the local overseers, to pronounce excommunications and refer recalcitrants to the civil courts. The behaviour, language and opinions of the citizens were subject to perpetual and ever-present inquisition. Penalties were exacted for purely religious or moral faults as well as for harmless games and even most innocent dances. From 1541 to 1546 alone fifty-eight death sentences were carried out and seventy-six people were banished.

History has recorded some of the outstanding trials:

Sebastian Castellion was deprived of his pastoral ministry because he had disagreed with Calvin on a biblical matter; Peter Ameaux, a member of the Little Council, was condemned to do penance in his shirt and carrying a candle in his hand, for having spoken ill of Calvin (1546); Franchequine Perrin, wife of the Captain-General, was imprisoned for dancing and for calling a minister a lewd fellow; James Gruet was beheaded in July, 1547, for having threatened Calvin and insisted on "the right to dance, jump and enjoy life"; Jerome Bolsec, a doctor, was banished for having rejected the doctrine of predestination (1551); lastly, and especially, Michael Servet, on October 27th, 1553, was burned for having denied the doctrine of the Holy Trinity.

We cannot speak of Calvin without recalling the doctrine to which he adhered above all others, which most vividly reflects his sombre and forceful spirit—his doctrine of predestination, taken from Luther, but made his own with singular intransigence. He defined it as follows: "We call predestination the eternal decision of God, whereby he has determined what he wishes to do with every man, for he does not create them all in like condition but foreordains some to eternal life and others to eternal damnation."

We may add that this dreadful doctrine, after provoking quarrels of unheard-of violence amongst the Calvinist churches, especially in Holland, ended by being rejected as immoral nearly a century ago, and it seems clearly to have been given up by everyone in the Protestant sects, whose tendency is rather to deny the eternity of the pains of hell and to revert to that universal restoration of which Origen spoke in the third century.[3]

[3] There is a special volume in this series on Protestantism.

CHAPTER VII

ANGLICANISM: A
PROFUSION OF SECTS

THE THIRTY-NINE ARTICLES

The Anglican Church forms a distinctive institution in the heart of Protestantism, a name which it repudiates but which is nevertheless often applied to it. King Henry VIII at first showed great hostility towards Lutheranism and obtained from the Holy See the title of "Defender of the Faith". But having failed to obtain from Rome the dissolution of his marriage with Catharine of Aragon or the recognition of his remarriage with Anne Boleyn, he proclaimed himself head of the Church of England. Catholics who remained faithful to Rome were condemned and executed as traitors to the Crown, whereas Lutheran heretics were burned. This is what is known as the Anglican schism (1534). It produce martyrs, of whom the two best known are John Fisher, Bishop of Rochester, and Thomas More, Chancellor of the realm.

After the death of Henry VIII, his son Edward VI succeeded to the throne, but as he was only ten years old, Somerset and, later, Warwick ruled as regents. It was during this regency that the Protestant heresy made its first appearance; its ring-leader was none other than Cranmer, whom Henry VIII had made archbishop of Canterbury and who had maintained an attitude of caution during the king's reign. From the Continent he brought over Martin Bucer of Strasbourg, the apostate Bernardino Ochino, a former General of the Capuchins, Peter Martyr, ex-Augustinian of Fiesole, and John Knox, the future "reformer" of Scotland.

The wind of heresy blew through the kingdom. Soon Calvin was sending long letters from Geneva, full of advice which purported to treat the young king as an accomplished theologian. By 1549 the English had at last learned what they were to believe; Cranmer published a Confession of faith in "Forty-two Articles".

Suddenly an unexpected event occurred in the death of the young king. His step-sister, Mary Tudor, daughter of Henry VIII by his first marriage, succeeded him. She had never ceased to be a Catholic and she immediately ordered the release from prison of Henry's bishops who had refused to subscribe to the Forty-two Articles of Cranmer. In his turn the latter was arrested and expiated his political and religious vacillations on the scaffold. Mary, aided by her cousin Cardinal Reginald Pole, reconciled England with Rome, and men now hoped for a return to peace and tranquillity, but on November 15th, 1558, Mary died, leaving no issue from her marriage with the King of Spain, Philip II (son of Charles V), a marriage greatly resented by the English people.

Queen Elizabeth, who succeeded Mary, was the daughter of Henry VIII and Anne Boleyn. She was a woman of character, cultured, determined and able to wield authority, but devoid of all moral sense and in addition cynical, cruel and addicted to coquetry. This was the woman who made the final breach with Rome and gave her realm its *Credo* and its organized religion. In 1559, by the Act of Supremacy, she proclaimed herself head of the national Church, while the Act of Uniformity rigorously enforced the use of the Book of Common Prayer which had already been published in the time of Edward VI.

All the bishops of Mary's reign were dismissed and a Calvinist, Matthew Parker, was appointed to the primatial see of Canterbury. In 1559 he was consecrated, invalidly according to Rome, because the idea of sacrifice, without which there is no true priesthood, was deliberately excluded from the Ordinal. And as Parker, being himself without the power to consecrate, subsequently consecrated all the other bishops according to this same invalid Ordinal, Anglican Orders were thenceforth invalid. After most careful research, necessitated out of respect for the profound convictions of certain Anglicans, Leo XIII was compelled to declare these ordinations invalid, in the Bull *Apostolicae curae* (September 13th, 1896).

As for the Confession of Faith, a return was made to the Forty-two Articles of Edward VI, but in 1563 their number was reduced to thirty-nine and these have remained the official charter of the Anglican Church. Of these Thirty-nine Articles some are orthodox, namely those on God, the Trinity, the Incarnation, the death and resurrection of Christ, the divinity of the Holy Spirit, the obligatory character of the decalogue and the Nicene and Athanasian Creeds. But there are others which have retained the heresies of Luther and Calvin: article six, which affirms that "Scripture contains all things necessary to salvation", and so leaves out "tradition" which, no less than the authority of the Church, is aided by the Holy Spirit. Article nine defines original sin as "the fault and corruption of the nature of every man . . . and this infection of nature doth remain . . . in them that are regenerated" (through baptism). It thus confuses sin with concupiscence, which is a consequence of it, and impairs the efficacy of baptism. Article eleven teaches justification by faith without works, which is frankly heretical. Article nineteen asserts that "the Church of Rome hath erred . . . in matters of faith". Article twenty-two professes to give some examples of these errors, such as belief in purgatory, the practice of indulgences, the veneration of images, relics and saints. Article twenty-five recognizes only two sacraments instead of seven, baptism and the Lord's Supper. And in the Lord's Supper the Anglican Church, like Calvin, admits only a spiritual presence of Christ, and that only at the moment of communion. Article thirty-one abolishes the Mass as the sacrifice of the new Law, and thirty-two does away with the celibacy of the clergy. It should be added that these articles have been, and still are, interpreted by Anglicans in very different ways, so that the Anglican Church contains groups whose theological ideas vary from complete radicalism to a position not far removed from Roman Catholicism.

So we find the "High Church", which is on the near brink of the Catholic Faith, the "Broad Church", which attaches little importance to dogmas and interprets them in the most liberal way possible, and the "Low Church", which is close to Calvinism and hostile to Rome.

THE MULTIPLICITY OF SECTS

These divergent views amongst Anglicans bring us to the far more serious fact of the profusion of sects which is the predominant feature of the story of Protestantism in its various forms. As a result of the principle of recourse to the Bible there arose almost everywhere, alongside the official, established churches, more or less virulent sects whose common feature was nonconformity. Biblicism has always acted as a centrifugal force, a ferment of disruption and division *ad infinitum*. This is observed, not only by all the great Catholic controversialists, and in particular Bossuet, in his famous and universally admired masterpiece of 1688, *History of the Variations of the Protestant Churches*; the same thing is observed by Protestant authors. A recent American writer, Charles Morrison, wrote: "The fissiparous tendency characteristic of all Protestantism, is truly excessive in the United States of America." The Annual of United States' Churches for 1954 lists no fewer than eighty-six different denominations. But even amongst these some are subdivided into numerous sects, so we may reckon on something like two hundred and sixty-three Protestant sects at present existing in the United

States, where all the European denominations are also represented with the consequent intensive tendency to divide. Here
is a summary list which may give some idea of this profusion
of religious groups, independent of one another:

Baptist Churches in the U.S.A.	17,470,111	members, in	29	sects.
Methodist ,,	,, 11,664,978	,,	,, 21	,,
Lutheran ,,	,, 6,313,892	,,	,, 19	,,
Presbyterian (Calvinists)	3,535,171	,,	,, 10	,,
Protestant (Episcopalian)	2,482,887	,, in a single sect.		
Disciples of Christ	1,815,627	,, ,,	,,	,,
Evangelical Churches	1,618,339	,,	,, 5	sects.
Church of Christ	1,500,000	,,	,, 1	sect.
Congregationalist Churches	1,273,628	,,	,, 2	sects.
Mormons, or Latter Day Saints	1,210,336	,,	,, 6	,,
Church of Christ Scientist	1,112,123	,,	,, 1	sect.

Besides these Churches of upwards of a million adherents,
but themselves frequently divided into more or less numerous
sects, there are in addition a great number of groups comprising only a few thousand members, but often making up
for their small numbers by the violence of their propaganda.

This multiplicity of sects is a feature of the present era. It
is generally agreed that the theology of most of these sects is
brimming with absurd ideas or extravagant hopes, but this
profusion must be considered as a revealing symptom. It indicates a topsy-turvy troubled world, seeking on all sides for a
glimmer of light, producing new messiahs and combining
extreme anxiety with illuminist forebodings.

Among the principal sects at work in Europe at the present
time are:

1. The Seventh Day Adventists, founded in 1833, with
about 113 churches and 8,000 members in Great Britain.

2. The Friends of Man, whose founder was a Swiss dentist,
A. Freytag, c. 1920. He called himself "the Messenger of the
Eternal". On his death two rival sects emerged from this
group.

3. Jehovah's Witnesses, the most virulent and dangerous of all these sects since it is organized more or less commercially and has considerable assets which enable it to conduct intensive propaganda. It was founded in the United States of America *c.* 1870 by C. T. Russell, as a result of a split from the Adventists and was reorganized by Judge Rutherford. The teaching is entirely alien to Christianity despite its biblical pretensions.

4. The Pentecostal Assemblies, deriving from a Californian revival at the beginning of the twentieth century, which rely particularly upon cells, not organized as churches properly so called, and insist on the "baptism of the spirit", and "enthusiasm". Its adherents rely on the Scriptures, every word of which is taken literally, and on the practice of the imposition of hands to cure every sickness.

5. Christian Science (Church of Christ, Scientist), which despite its name is neither Christian nor scientific; founded *c.* 1879 by the American, Mrs Eddy; it is devoted especially to healing illness by auto-suggestion, which the sect calls mind cure. In the United States, where its centre is at Boston, it has acquired considerable importance, but it has encountered less success abroad, especially on the continent of Europe.

There are also certain sects with few members such as the Church of the Living God, which numbers one hundred and twenty members in six congregations, the Church of St Mary the Virgin, which has only eight hundred members in one congregation. Certain other sects have been reduced to very small proportions, e.g. the Quakers or Shakers, of whom we shall speak later.

It is clearly almost impossible to find a doctrine common to all these sects. We shall, however, try to indicate their chief tendencies together with some notes on their histories.

DOCTRINES AND TENDENCIES

We have given sufficient indications of the doctrines professed by the great "established" Protestant Churches,
Lutheran, Calvinist and Anglican. It must never be forgotten
that within these same Churches orthodoxy properly so called
no longer exists. The principle of private judgement functions
in every one of them. We have seen that three tendencies
exist in the established Church of England, and that very considerable differences are to be found within the same denomi-
nation, marking off the High Church from the Broad and
from the Low Church. In the Calvinist Church of Geneva we
find the same thing. As in parliamentary assemblies, there
can be distinguished a conservative right wing, an advanced
progressive left and a moderate centre. The constitution of
this Church lays down that "each pastor teaches and preaches
the Gospel freely on his own responsibility; this freedom cannot be restricted either by confessions of faith or by liturgical
formulas".

This freedom of conduct is still more evident in the dissident sects. It follows that doctrinal contacts are sometimes
very slight; all the sects, however, believe in one God. Only
the Christian Scientists profess this belief in God in the form
of pantheism. Most Protestants admit the Trinity, yet since
the sixteenth century, after the Italian Protestants Laelius and
Faustus Socinus (the Latinized forms of Lelio and Fausto
Sozzini), the Unitarians have rejected this dogma. The most
illustrious adherent of this sect was undoubtedly the American
writer and thinker Emerson (1803–82). On the Incarnation,
while all Protestants recite the Creed as Catholics do, there
are some, particularly among the Congregationalists, who go
back to the sixteenth century, who are modalists, that is, attribute the Incarnation to a mode of being of the Godhead
without distinction of the Person who is incarnate.

On the subject of the sacraments Protestants generally

admit baptism and the Lord's Supper, but while some continue to profess the necessity of baptism for salvation others do not regard it as indispensable. The Baptists, who derive from the Anabaptists contemporary with Luther, refuse baptism to infants, teaching that it can only be conferred upon adults. In the matter of the Eucharist all Protestants reject transubstantiation in the Catholic sense. However, Lutherans and a good number of Anglicans admit the real Presence. Calvinists, on the other hand, believe only in a spiritual presence dependent upon the faith of the communicant.

For the matter of the sacrament, some use unleavened bread, as we do, but the majority use ordinary leavened bread; there are much more important differences in the wine used; some use it as Christ did and as we do (Episcopalians and Lutherans or Calvinists), others replace this by unfermented grape juice (Methodists); others again will use only pure water (Mormons and others).

On the question of ecclesiastical discipline, all Protestants reject the authority of the pope—one of the rare points on which they are all agreed—but Episcopalians and Lutherans admit the legitimacy and even the necessity of the episcopate, while Presbyterians, who are Calvinists, insist that the episcopate is a human invention, a product of non-primitive Christianity, and Congregationalists reject all authority apart from the whole congregation or assembly of the faithful.

RATIONALISM AND ILLUMINISM

The tendencies within Protestantism, considered either historically or at the present time, may be seen to reveal two opposite extremes, rationalist on the one hand and illuminist on the other. Rationalism tends to reduce everything to the level of reason and to interpret even Scripture as a function of human philosophy or of changeable scientific data. Understood in this sense it can be said that rationalism has been one of the most consistent temptations of Protestantism. Some

noted theologians like Schleiermacher, David Strauss, Albert
Ritschl, Adolph Harnack, Albert Réville and some dozen or
so others, who have made a name in exegesis or in history,
were straightforward rationalists. A century ago Protestantism
was imbued with rationalism. The Christian religion was
thereby reduced to sentiment or to almost entirely profane
philosophical views. Thus in our own times German or Dutch
exegesis is strongly tainted by rationalism, in the sense that
it is averse to admitting anything which goes beyond reason,
such as prophecy properly so called or the miraculous.

At the opposite extreme to this widespread rationalism
Protestantism is often affected, both in the past and today, by
a pronounced tendency to illuminism. We have already mentioned the Quakers—whose name means shakers or tremblers
by reason of their state of exaltation in prayer. They were
founded in the seventeenth century by the Englishman,
George Fox (1624–91), but their chief theologian was Robert
Barclay (1648–90). Fox, who was not well educated, appealed,
without being aware of it, to reason and inspiration. "It is
repeatedly stated," he said, "that Christ said this, the apostles
said that. But what do you yourselves say? Are you a son of
the light? Have you walked in the way of light, and does
what you say come to you directly from God?" This individual inspiration could equally well be personal imagination
or human reasoning; it was sufficient to attribute it to God
speaking directly to the soul for it to be believed.

Others, like the Mormons, who were founded by one Joseph
Smith (1805–44), add what they call "The Book of the Mormons" to the Bible; this book purported to have been brought
to Smith in 1830 by two angels. So they say: "We believe that
the Bible is the Word of God in so far as it has been correctly
translated; however we hold that the Book of the Mormons
is the Word of God." Here the neo-revelation occupies such
a large place in relation to the Bible that in this sort of
Protestantism we can speak of Christianity as being reduced
to a vestigial state or a remote memory.

Illuminism within the Protestant Churches has taken many forms. One of the most interesting of these was the common practice of the revival. Briefly, it is a question of something truly Christian, for revival in itself is nothing else than conversion. But the name revivalism is given particularly to mass conversions. The Catholic Church has known such conversions, by popular preachers like Vincent Ferrer, Bernardine of Siena, John of Capistran and, nearer to our own times, Fr de Maunoir, Francis Régis, Grignion de Montfort and Leonard of Port Maurice.

PIETISM

With the technique of revivalism must be associated two of the most powerful movements which have marked the story of Protestantism; the Pietism of the seventeenth century and the Methodism of the eighteenth. The characteristic of movements of this sort is a reaction, analogous to that which we see today in the influence of Karl Barth and under the hand of Kierkegaard, but far more popular and far stronger, against a religion which has become too formalistic, mechanical and commonplace. Pietism, under the impulse of Philip Jakob Spener (1635–1705), established *Collegia pietatis*—hence the name—where men gathered to read the Bible, sing psalms and practise what they called "true Christianity" as opposed to ordinary and commonplace Christianity.

His most formidable opponent in the sixteenth century was the Lutheran theologian Valentine Löscher, who criticized him on the following points: (1) doctrinal indifference masked by piety; (2) contempt of the sacraments by appeal to personal inspiration; (3) lack of respect for the pastoral ministry in reducing it to certain slavish forms of piety; (4) confusion of faith with works which accompany faith and justification; (5) a tendency towards Millenarianism; (6) limitation of the efficacy of divine grace; (7) meticulousness in condemning immaterial things, or *adiaphora*; (8) a tendency towards mysticism; (9) abolition of the religious aids to be obtained from the visible Church, confessions of faith, liturgical rules, in favour of recourse to individual inspiration; (10) indulgence towards all the illuminist sects which Lutheranism had always condemned; (11) the claim of "perfectionism" which calls for the "total destruction of the old Adam" and makes the Christian life consist in the growth of interior faith; (12) "reformism" which casts scorn on the ordinary Church and will recognize it only among the "regenerated"; (13) evident and troublesome separatism.

Pietism had certainly a tendency to despise profoundly the common herd of Christians whom we should today call *bien pensants*. Pietism has remained a tendency within Lutheranism but it is still a purely individual phenomenon.

METHODISM

There is undoubtedly a relationship between Germanic pietism and English Methodism. Methodism is derived from the two Wesley brothers, John and Charles. The former (1703–81) began his activities during his second year at Oxford in 1729. He gathered a few friends for Bible reading, pious exercises, works of charity and fasting. They were derisively called "Bible moths", or "the holy club", and eventually Methodists, that is, those who practised a method of sanctity.

The two Wesleys and their friend George Whitefield threw themselves into preaching and soon achieved enormous popular success. They were chiefly opposed by the Anglican clergy, and by force of circumstances were obliged to preach outside churches, sometimes in schools, sometimes in the open air. But while Whitefield remained attached to the Calvinistic doctrine of predestination the Wesleys, separating from him, remained within the Anglican fold as a kind of special sect. Whitefield, aided by Griffith Jones, Howell Harris and Daniel Rowland, with the support of the Countess of Huntingdon, organized a distinct Church which became the Presbyterian Church of Wales. John Wesley, for his part, being deprived of Anglican ministers by the ill-will of the clergy of his Church, performed ordinations himself and ended—especially in his American branch—by breaking away entirely from the Anglicanism in which he had begun. However, he remained faithful to a great extent to the Thirty-nine Articles of the Church of his birth, though he reduced these articles to twenty-five in his own creed. The great revivalist movements, either in the heart of Pietism or amongst the Methodists, have certainly produced a re-awakening of the Christian faith and brought a large number of souls to piety and the interior life. But it is equally undeniable that they have shown a tendency to minimize the importance of dogma and to reduce religion either to sentiment or to an almost entirely natural religion, accompanied by various good works. We find these traits in the Salvation Army, which is without doubt a remarkable philanthropic work, but is also a sort of permanent revival brought about by more or less sound methods. Among the most noxious sects noticed above, as for example the Adventists and Pentecostals, there is continually to be encountered the same kinds of tendencies, and inevitably comparison is invited with others in history, Montanism of the second century, Catharism of the twelfth, Quakerism of the seventeenth, the prophesying of the Camisards in France or the Jansenist convulsionism of the eighteenth century at the tomb of the deacon Pâris.

CONCLUSION

At the end of this short account of heresies something will be said about the attempts made by ecumenicism to restore that Christian unity so tragically broken by the Protestant revolution. It must suffice in conclusion here to mention that many enlightened Protestants refuse to recognize any authentic Christianity in the sects; for them these sects are "heresies". One of the leading dignitaries of the reformed Church of France recently remarked: "You would never believe what a service the Reformation rendered to the Catholic Church; it has relieved her of heresies, and we have inherited them!"

We shall see in the next chapter that this statement is not altogether true.

CHAPTER VIII

JANSENISM, OR THE
THIRD REFORM

MICHAEL BAIUS, THE FORERUNNER OF JANSENISM

The heart-rending example of the Protestant secession has made it abundantly clear that those who wish to "reform" the Church must not begin by breaking away from her. And those who intend to reform her belief or institutions are frequently eager to remain within her fold. Such was the case with the Jansenists. Before describing the origin of this insidious heresy we must briefly recall the attempt, which quickly miscarried, on the part of Michael de Bay, known as Baius. For a long time it was thought that there was a direct relationship between Baianism and Jansenism; today it is not quite so clear. But that there was some relationship or similarity between the two movements is undeniable. Michael de Bay, a native of Hainaut, was born in 1513. In 1542 we find him as a professor of philosophy at Louvain, and in 1552 as a professor of exegesis. Before long he was blamed for dubious teaching on the primitive state of man, and on grace and freedom. Beginning in 1563 he published a series of small tracts on these questions. Eventually, on October 1st, 1567, a Bull of Pius V condemned seventy-nine propositions drawn from his works. After several attempts to turn this condemnation to his advantage, he was again condemned by

Gregory XIII in 1579. He submitted, and became chancellor
of the University of Louvain until his death in 1589. What
were these propositions which were censured by the Church?
According to Baius man was not created in a supernatural
state. All the gifts which we call supernatural or preter-
natural in Adam—the right to the beatific vision of God, the
adoptive sonship of man through sanctifying grace, exemp-
tion from suffering and death, infused knowledge—were gifts
due to nature. It follows that original sin was a corruption of
nature itself and not the privation of supernatural and preter-
natural gifts. Henceforth, man is incapable of any good without grace, he is the slave of sin. His freedom is purely
external, for he is tyrannized interiorly by an irresistible concupiscence, although this, according to Baius, does not relieve
him of his responsibility. These views, without Baius being
aware of it, were purely and simply a return to the heresy of
Luther and Calvin. Thus Baianism is held to be semi-
Protestantism.

JANSEN AND THE AUGUSTINUS

Cornelius Jansen was also a doctor of Louvain, but he did
not know Baius and does not seem to have been influenced
by him. He was born in 1585 at Acquoy in the diocese of
Utrecht (Holland). He was a studious, very moral and well-
read man. After his studies at Louvain he made the acquain-
tance in Paris of a young French cleric named Duvergier de
Hauranne, who took him to his mother's estate in the immediate neighbourhood of Bayonne. For several years the two
friends, the cold, calm Dutchman and the ardent, effervescent
Basque, worked together, steeping themselves in the works of
the Fathers. Then Jansen returned home where he at once
became superior of a college in Louvain, doctor of that university and a man held in high esteem for his immense
patristic learning. Jansen, whose name was Latinized as Jansenius, remained closely in touch with his friend, who for
his part had become Abbé de Saint-Cyran.

At this juncture (that is, about 1620) Jansenius became aware that before him no one had really understood St Augustine nor, consequently, the problems of grace and justification. An astonishing letter to his friend Saint-Cyran, dated March 5th, 1621, announced the great discovery. But as discussions on the matter of grace had been made subject by Rome to preliminary censorship, following controversies between Thomists and Molinists, he told his friend that he was going to pursue his studies, of which he would inform him confidentially, and in absolute secrecy in order to avoid premature condemnation. But he would clarify this whole question of grace and predestination out of St Augustine, at the same time differing from current teaching on the subject. "I dare to say," he wrote, "that I have discovered enough from immutable principles that when both schools of Jesuits and Jacobins (Dominicans) have argued until the day of judgement, following the lines on which they have begun, they will do nothing but lose themselves completely, both being a hundred leagues from the truth."

He added that he did not dare tell anybody his views about St Augustine for fear of being censured by Rome before the matter was ripe. Thus he embarked upon a course of secrecy. The two friends met at Louvain to arrange details and agreed on a code to use in their letters. The subject of grace according to St Augustine became for them Pilmot. Jansenius called himself sometimes Boèce (Boethius), sometimes Quinquarbre or Sulpice. Saint-Cyran was Celias, or Durillon or Solion. The Jesuits, of whom both had been pupils or friends, became for them what we should call "Enemy number one", and were referred to as Gorphoroste, or Pacuvius or "the ends". St Augustine was called Seraphi, Leoninus, Aelius. Domini meant the Court of Rome, Purpuratus was Richelieu, etc. This extensive use of conventional expressions seems unusual enough to us but it indicates clearly the strange and presumptuous character of the affair. Who would have believed that Augustine could have remained unknown to everyone until

Jansenius? Who could have imagined in any case that his teaching, if it had remained unknown to everybody, was so indispensable to the good of the Church? Even Sante-Beuve was astonished at it. Speaking of St Augustine, he exclaims: "This, then, must take the place of St Paul, it is almost on a par with the Gospel. . . . Can we allow this?"

But Jansenius pursued blindly the path he had made for himself; he persevered until his death. In 1636, he became bishop of Ypres, and died two years later, leaving to the two friends whom he had entrusted with its publication, the manuscript of his huge work entitled *Augustinus*, with all paper for printing it and the necessary instructions.

SAINT-CYRAN

When Jansenius died on May 6th, 1638, his friend Saint-Cyran in Paris was on the point of being thrown into prison by the terrible Purpuratus, Richelieu. He was arrested and put in the dungeon of Vincennes on May 14th, 1635, but for what crime? In reality, it was purely for reasons of state. Richelieu saw him as a good man, in the front rank of learning, but also as a dangerous man capable of upsetting the State by upsetting the Church. Duvergier de Hauranne is in fact one of the most curious figures in history. St Francis de Sales held him in high esteem, as did St Vincent de Paul. Truth to tell, his earlier writings had not given the impression of a well-balanced mind, but later he published two works in which he castigated the Jesuits, his former masters, in a high-handed manner, under the veil of anonymity which was quickly pierced by knowledgeable people. Above all, he had defended the nuns of Port-Royal at an awkward moment, when one of their devotions called the Secret Chaplet had been criticized and ridiculed. At the beginning of Lent, 1635, Saint-Cyran, defender of the Secret Chaplet, became the official director and confessor of the famous monastery of Port-Royal, destined to become an impregnable fortress for

him, thanks to the Arnauld family which formed a real and
closely united clan. Saint-Cyran's success at Port-Royal was
immediate and complete. The most tractable, avid and sym-
pathetic supporter of the new director's ideas was the Abbess,
Mother Angélique Arnauld. And at once the great name of
St Augustine seemed to brood over the convent. In such
circumstances Richelieu's decision against Saint-Cyran in
1638, far from diminishing his prestige, added to his reputation the halo of confessor of the faith.

THE AUGUSTINUS

Saint-Cyran had been at Vincennes for two years, whence
he continued to direct the souls of his male and female ad-
mirers, when his friend Jansenius's enormous book made its
appearance. Before reading it, Saint-Cyran took it under his
protection and all his supporters followed him eagerly. The
book was submitted to the judgement of the Holy See. Before
any intervention on the part of Rome Saint-Cyran proclaimed that the book would be "the devotional book of the
last days". When anyone spoke to him of the probability of
opposition by the Sorbonne he exclaimed heatedly that "it
was a book which would last as long as the Church". And
he added with an assurance that astounded anyone with some
idea of the guidance of the Church by the Holy Spirit, that "if
the king and the pope combined to destroy it, it was done in
such a way that they would never succeed".

Saint-Cyran, then, went further than Jansenius himself,
who at least submitted in advance to the pope's judgement.
It can no longer be contested that Saint-Cyran was the chief
author of the Jansenist heresy for without him the *Augustinus*
would have been still-born, a book which Rome's censures
might have stopped in its course on the day it was published.
Instead it was propagated widely and eagerly devoured,
despite its forbidding dryness, and republished in France
before Rome could intervene. And when Saint-Cyran (re-

leased from prison a few months after Richelieu's death) died on October 11th, 1643, fortified by the last rites and attended by his parish priest, he had time to pass on the torch to a talented priest, the brother of Mother Angélique, Antoine Arnauld, a brilliant teacher of Augustinianism, as understood by Jansenius.

ANTOINE ARNAULD AND FREQUENT COMMUNION

With Arnauld, Jansenism enters a new phase. It will be noted that it had still not been denounced and condemned as a heresy. Jansenius and Saint-Cyran both died in the peace of the Church; they believed themselves to be not only her faithful and submissive sons, but also her benefactors and almost her reformers. But Rome, having forbidden the discussion of controversial questions concerning grace without special authorization, condemned the *Augustinus* without any searching examination. Saint-Cyran launched his cherished disciple Antoine Arnauld along a quite new path which, unlike grace, had not been forbidden. And before his death he had time to approve the book, *On Frequent Communion* (1643), which had sprung from his own counsel and example. This book was to endow Jansenism with its second dominant feature. Later we shall see that the first feature was a merciless doctrinal rigorism which removed all efficacy of human freedom in order to attribute everything to the action of grace. The second feature, not unconnected with the first, was a moral rigorism abounding with requirements of exacting severity. Under these two related and converging aspects Jansenism merited the name of revived Calvinism which has sometimes been given to it. Jansenist rigorism is in fact the counterpart of Calvinist puritanism just as its doctrine of irresistible grace is the counterpart of the dogma of predestination. The Calvinists were well aware of this, for they welcomed the *Augustinus* with open arms.

The chief peculiarity of Arnauld's book on frequent communion is that it contrives to recommend frequent communion while hedging it around with so many considerations, conditions and safeguards that in the end it acts as a deterrent rather than as an encouragement. But this was not Antoine Arnauld's principal service in support of Jansenism and its continuance. He brought to the service of the heresy stupendous talents of subtlety, extreme competence and tenacity and, it must be admitted, deceit and guile. By his doing the heresy became elusive and evasive. And as he had behind him the entire monastery of Port-Royal, filled with his close relations and friends, and a whole host of noble personages, of virtue and ability, attracted by the solitude of the place since the days of Saint-Cyran, Jansenism was practically invincible and ineradicable. The judgements of the Church glided over it without affecting it or even seriously impairing it. It only disappeared finally as a result of the evolution of ideas which its twofold rigorism has encountered among most of our contemporaries.

THE FIVE PROPOSITIONS

The excitement caused by Arnauld's book resulted in his having to take refuge for a time "under God's wings", that is, among his friends. Meanwhile, the Sorbonne had at last sifted through the enormous *Augustinus*. At a meeting on July 1st, 1649, the *syndic* of the Sorbonne, Nicolas Cornet, denounced seven propositions extracted from Jansenius' book. After discussions, these seven propositions, alleged to be a summary of the thesis of the book, were reduced to five and submitted to Rome. It is important to note that no one at the outset disputed that the five propositions were an accurate abstract of the new doctrine. This is proved by the fact that the Jansenist party immediately sent its best doctors—proudly parading the title of "Augustinians"—to defend them before the Holy See. The examination of the Court of Rome was long and thorough, as was customary, and there was ample time to discover whether the five propositions were in fact to be found in the *Augustinus*. The point is emphasized here because it was afterwards questioned—an outrageous equivocation whose consequences we shall see.

In spite of all the speeches of the "Augustinians", the Five Propositions were condemned by the Bull *Cum Occasione*, dated May 31st, 1653, published in Rome on June 9th on the high authority of Innocent X. This condemnation was renewed under Alexander VII on October 16th, 1656, by the Bull *Ad sanctam B. Petri Sedem* and later still by the Bull *Vineam Domini* of Clement XI, on July 15th, 1705. The very number of these repeated condemnations emphasizes the continual attempts of the Jansenists to elude the authority of the Church.

The following are the celebrated and much controverted Five Propositions:

1. Some of God's commandments are impossible to just men who wish and strive (to keep them), considering the powers they actually have; the grace by which these precepts may become possible is also wanting.
2. In the state of fallen nature no one ever resists interior grace.
3. To merit, or demerit, in the state of fallen nature, we must be free from all external constraint, but not from interior necessity.
4. The Semi-Pelagians admitted the necessity of interior preventing grace for all acts, even for the beginning of faith; but they fell into heresy in pretending that this grace is such that man may either follow or resist it.
5. To say that Christ died or shed his blood for all men is Semi-Pelagianism.

Theologically these propositions were qualified as (1) Temerarious, impious, blasphemous, heretical; (2) Heretical; (3) Heretical; (4) Historically false and heretical; (5) Historically false, rash, scandalous and, understood in the sense that

Christ died only for the predestined, impious, blasphemous, insulting towards God and heretical.

The first reaction in the Jansenist party, notably at Port-Royal, was one of dismay, but also of rejection of the condemnation on the grounds of the intrigues and plots of the "Molinists", that is, the Jesuits at the Court of Rome. Instead of accepting the condemnation and submitting, they concentrated on the detailed side of the affair; thus from being a heresy about grace it imperceptibly evolved into a heresy about the Church.

RIGHT AND FACT

But two years later, only two years later, Arnauld had what could be called a stroke of genius, unparalleled in the history of heresy. Never had it occurred to Wyclif, John Huss, Luther or Baius to declare, "I condemn what the Church condemns, but that is not my doctrine." In his *Seconde Lettre à un Duc et Pair* (Second Letter to a Duke and Peer) in 1655 (July 10th), Arnauld doubted whether the Five Propositions were to be found in Jansenius and vindicated the *Augustinus*. He was immediately attacked by the Sorbonne for this Letter; he retracted, but was none the less excluded from the Faculty. The definitive censure was pronounced against him on January 31st, 1656, causing him to lose all his privileges as a *socius sorbonicus*. In order to avoid this censure he had nevertheless given evidence in writing that "he condemned the Five Propositions in any book in which they were found without exception, including that of Jansenius". The mistake was made of not being satisfied with this explanation; this revived the whole controversy more strongly than ever. Arnauld never ceased to maintain these two points, "We condemn the Five Propositions"—that was the question of right—"but they are not to be found in Jansenius"—that was the question of fact.

Arnauld also maintained that the Church may properly make pronouncements on the question of right and is thereby exercising her infallibility, but that she cannot make pronouncements on the question of fact so that in this case the only obligation is one of respectful silence.

THE PROVINCIALES

The confusion reached its peak through the publication, begun on January 23rd, 1656 (eight days before Arnauld's exclusion from the Sorbonne), of letters written to a Jesuit "provincial"; these were written in such a novel, brisk and convincing manner that the general public was suddenly swung round to favouring Jansenism. These letters, to the number of eighteen, which form a landmark in the history of French prose, were the work of a young mathematician, Blaise Pascal. They are no more than a collection of pamphlets in which truth is not entirely respected either in quotations, opinions or doctrine; but they were trenchant. It seems that Pascal subsequently regretted them and realized that his friends had made him play a part unworthy of his genius. In fact he died a few years later, fully reconciled to the Church from which, in thought, he had never been separated. But he achieved two distinct goals and inflicted wounds which have never been completely healed; on the one hand he cheerfully and mercilessly mocked at the discussions of the Sorbonne and at the clumsy scholastic trappings of theological usage. On the other hand he conducted against casuistry—of which rightly or wrongly he was pleased to attribute a monopoly to the Jesuits—such a lively and often irrefutably just offensive that he caused the name of Jesuitry to become synonymous with duplicity and pharisaism. The *Provinciales*, as Pascal's letters are called, is an immortal but biased book constituting only one episode in the story of one of the most subtle heresies which has left its mark on the pages of history.

THE FORMULARY

In order to put an end to these controversies which had become so strangely wearisome, the Assembly of the Clergy of France conceived the idea of drawing up a formulary which would be imposed on all members of the clergy, and on the monasteries and convents of the realm. But without any examination and knowing nothing of the implications of the question, the nuns of Port-Royal, basing their attitude on this distinction of right and fact which the formulary expressly intended to destroy, prepared themselves for a desperate resistance, as for martyrdom in times of persecution. In vain the archbishop of Paris, Hardouin de Beaumont de Péréfixe, came in person to call upon the religious to sign the formulary as had been done everywhere else in the realm.

In vain did he prevail upon Abbé Bossuet who, though still comparatively young, already had a reputation as one of the best minds among the French clergy, to explain it to them. They resolutely declined to submit and allowed themselves to be excommunicated on June 9th, 1664, as a kind of "conscientious objection". They remained steadfast in their obstinacy until an agreement, known to history as the Clementine Peace—after Clement IX—was made in February, 1669, applying to religious. This time the signatories "condemned the Five Propositions in all sincerity, without exception or reservation of any sort, in every sense in which the Church has condemned them". But by a new application of "Jesuitry", in the Pascalian sense, they implied that none of the opinions condemned by the Church was to be found in Jansenius whom indeed they had not read, but who had been a friend of their greatly revered hero, Saint-Cyran.

To finish the story of these nuns, it may be added that they were once again implicated in Jansenist controversy and that Port-Royal was eventually demolished by order of Louis XIV. and all the nuns were sent away on October 29th, 1709.

At that date Arnauld, nicknamed "the great Arnauld" by his followers, had been dead since August 8th, 1694, and Jansenism had found its third leader in the person of Fr Pasquier Quesnel of the Oratory.

QUESNEL AND THE BULL UNIGENITUS

In his youth Quesnel had studied at the Sorbonne and had been among the small number of opponents of the censures inflicted on Jansenism and Antoine Arnauld. Thus he was deeply imbued with the Jansenist spirit, frequenting only masters of his own choosing and shutting out all other influences. Born in Paris on July 14th, 1634, he was only twenty-eight when in 1662 he wrote his Moral Reflections on each verse of the Gospels, but the book only appeared in 1671 under the title: *Abrégé de la Morale de l'Evangile* ("Summary of the Moral Philosophy of the Gospels"). When the book was condemned by Clement X in 1675, Quesnel returned to it, amplified it, and republished it in four volumes under a new title: *Le Nouveau Testament avec les Réflexions morales* ("The New Testament with some Moral Reflections"). By practising "Jesuitry" he found a way of signing all the formularies required of him by his Congregation without in any way changing any of his private views. Following the second publication of his book he was banished from Paris to Orléans, by order of the archbishop of Paris, and subsequently expelled from the Oratory in 1684. The next year he left for Belgium and, hiding under a false name, lived with his master, Antoine Arnauld, one of the patriarchs of Jansenism, was present at his deathbed and succeeded him as leader of the party.

In the summer of 1701 discussions about "right and fact", which might be thought to have been resolved, began once more in connection with the "Case of Conscience"; could one, without believing in the *fact*, on the question of the *Augustinus*, and without admitting that the Church had the

JANSENISM, OR THE THIRD REFORM

right to exact belief on this point, still sign the formulary, maintaining a respectful silence, and so obtain absolution?

In the Sorbonne the "Case", at first received by the agreement of forty doctors, was later criticized by others, referred to Rome and condemned on February 12th, 1703. A little later Fr Quesnel was found in Brussels on May 30th, 1703, arrested and put into prison, and all his papers were seized. When these papers were sent to the court of France they revealed a new conspiracy, analogous to that which Jansenius had nicknamed Pilmot. They too treated all matters under fictitious names, which became a traditional method of the sect. Quesnel's papers were decoded, carefully examined, summarized and placed before the king of France, who for years had entertained strong hostility towards Jansenism. Every evening for ten years Louis XIV had these documents read to him, and they never failed to provoke him to repressions which were long overdue.

The king pressed Clement XI to issue a Bull renewing all the previous condemnations of the heresy in question. The pope acquiesced, and on July 16th, 1705, published the Constitution called *Vineam Domini Sabaoth*. This decided against the Case of Conscience and ruled that respectful silence on matters condemned by the Church was not sufficient and that an interior compliance must be added by acknowledging that Jansenius's book was actually tainted with heresy.

It was precisely on account of their refusal to accept this new Bull that the nuns of Port-Royal were expelled from their convent and that the latter was demolished by royal orders. But the very resistance of the nuns and the sympathy with which they met gave the king proof that Jansenism still retained adherents. Anxious to abolish it entirely he made a further request to the pope, asking him solemnly to condemn the errors contained in Quesnel's book "Moral Reflections". Once again the pope concurred with the king's views, which were more than justified in the event. On September 8th, 1713, appeared the celebrated Bull *Unigenitus*, which was to stir up so long and so terrible a storm but was also to reveal at the same time the extent of the ravages caused by Jansenism in the Church.

THE BULL UNIGENITUS AND NEO-JANSENISM

Quesnel's Jansenism may be called Neo-Jansenism because it manifested a new trend. Instead of being exhibited in the form of a well-knit system either in an imposing work like the *Augustinus*, or in the numerous works of Arnauld, it was insinuated into the texts of the New Testament in the form of a discreet commentary which was often edifying and even hyper-mystical and was pleasing in style. The Jansenist Batterel could say of Quesnel: "There was never a pen at the Oratory which has written about God in such a noble, exalted and illuminating manner and, I may add, so purely and so elegantly." Yet scrutiny of some reflection of Quesnel's reveals the original Jansenist hallmark which the Church had condemned as heresy. The very number of the propositions affected by the Bull *Unigenitus*—101 in place of only five condemned in the *Augustinus*—bears witness to this difference of presentation. But looked at closely we find those five amongst the 101, just as if the Church had not spoken at all.

For example, on the irresistible nature of grace: "Grace is the operation of the hand of the almighty God, which nothing can hinder or retard" (Proposition 10 of Quesnel). "When God wills to save a soul and touches it by the interior hand of his grace, no human will resists him" (Prop. 15). "There are no attractions that do not yield to the attraction of grace, for nothing resists the almighty" (Prop. 16).

On the total corruption of man after the Fall: "Without grace we can love nothing unless it is for our condemnation" (Prop. 40). "The prayer of the unrighteous is a new sin and what God grants them is a fresh judgement against them" (Prop. 59). That Jesus Christ did not die for all men: "Jesus Christ submitted to death to deliver his first-born (that is, the elect) in his blood for ever, from the hand of the destroying angel" (Prop. 32).

A good number of the condemned propositions were aimed at inculcating the Lutheran conception of the invisible Church. There was little mention of the visible Church except to annul the effects of "unjust" censures. Here is a series of Quesnel's propositions in this sense: "The mark of the Christian Church is to be Catholic in that she comprises all the angels in heaven and all the elect and the righteous on earth in every age" (Prop. 72). "What is the Church, if she is not the assembly of the sons of God living within her, adopted in Christ, submitting in his person, redeemed by his blood, acting by his grace and awaiting the grace of the world to come?" (73). "The Church, or the whole Christ, has the incarnate Word as her head, and all true saints as her members" (74). "The Church is a single man, composed of several members of which Christ is the head, the life, the subsistence and the person; there is only one Christ composed of a great multitude of saints, of whom he is the Sanctifier" (75). "Nothing is so vast as the Church of God, for she is composed of all the elect and all the righteous of every age" (76). "Whoso does not lead a life worthy of a son of God and a member of Christ ceases interiorly to have God for father and Christ as head" (77). In all these propositions we see that the Church is limited to the righteous and the elect, and sinners are excluded. The vast majority, not only of mankind but even of Christians, are thrown into outer darkness. Conversely, Quesnel desires it to be impossible to exclude him personally and his own party from the Church. "The Church" (says Propositions 90) "has the power of excommunication, to be exercised by her chief pastors with at least the presumed consent of the whole body." "The fear of unjust excommunication ought never to hinder us from doing our duty; we never leave the Church even when we seem to be driven out by the wickedness of man, so long as we remain attached by charity to God, to Jesus Christ and to the Church herself" (91).

THE APPELLANTS

The Bull *Unigenitus* raised a tremendous storm; it must be realized that all the events summarized here were accompanied by a deluge of publications, attacks and counter-attacks, explanations, apologies, commentaries, apologias and criticisms in every direction. And as Catholics were often restrained by the prohibition against writing on these matters, the initiative very often remained with the Jansenists and their friends, and this caused it to be said that their opponents preferred recourse to force or to censures rather than to valid arguments. The Jansenists jealously retained the same "superiority complex" which Luther had propagated by his *mystique* of consolation, Calvin by the *mystique* of election and puritanism, and Jansenius, Saint-Cyran and Arnauld in the name of "Augustinians" which they so proudly flourished. The disciples of Quesnel, wrapped up in their rigorism and their moral austerity, boasted of being the only members of the true Church, the Church of the elect and of the true saints.

The Bull however had been accepted by the vast majority of the clergy of France. Only four bishops appealed to a general council, and these were nicknamed the "Appellants". The *Libertés Gallicanes* came to be closely bound up with Jansenism. Theological Gallicanism, differing from parliamentary Gallicanism, asserted that only the decisions of an ecumenical council are irreformable. The archbishop of Paris, Noailles, the Gallican universities of Paris and Nantes, a large number of religious and some bishops came to strengthen the Appellants' party. The pope excommunicated them in 1718; they replied by renewing their appeal. Disorder soon reached a peak, the more so as the French Parliament sided with and championed the cause of the Jansenists.

THE CONVULSIONS OF SAINT-MÉDARD

Here passing reference may be made to the ridiculous episode of the convulsions of Saint-Médard which occurred between 1727 and 1732 at the tomb of the deacon Pâris, one of the glories of the sect, in the cemetery of Saint-Médard in Paris. Fanatical devotees who had come to pray at this tomb claimed to fall into ecstasy, allowed themselves to be trodden underfoot and beaten with iron bars without feeling any pain. The Jansenists claimed this to be miraculous, but intelligent persons attributed it to fraud or madness. The cemetery was closed in 1732 by royal command. But the "convulsions" and "miracles" continued behind closed doors, nourished by semi-secret literature on which the Jansenists thrived until the horrors of the French Revolution.

THE AFFAIR OF THE REFUSAL OF THE SACRAMENTS

After 1731 the struggle, which continued to be bitter on both sides, entered a new phase through the affair of the refusal of the sacraments. The Catholic clergy excluded obdurate and impenitent Appellants from communion; the latter brought legal actions against priests who refused them the consolations of religion. Parliamentary judges regularly condemned these priests who were faithful to the Church's discipline. Then the royal authority over-ruled the parliamentary sentences as tainted with illegality and injustice. This conflict lasted for twenty-five years until Benedict XIV succeeded in 1756 in putting an end to it by ruling that only notorious Appellants should be deprived of the sacraments. Parliament had to accept this papal decision under royal pressure, but did so with bad grace.

FROM UTRECHT TO PISTOIA

In concluding this all too brief summary of an endless and inglorious struggle, we may mention that if France was spared schism, properly so called, this was not the case abroad. A schismatic Jansenist Church was formed at Utrecht in Holland, where it still exists. Quesnel in fact escaped from his prison in Brussels and took refuge in Utrecht. He died at Amsterdam on December 2nd, 1719, but he had propagated his ideas sufficiently widely for a separation from Rome to take place after his death. In 1723, the Jansenists elected a certain Cornelius Steenoven as dissident archbishop of Utrecht, and obtained his valid consecration by Dominique Varlet, a bishop suspended in 1725; then, to ensure the succession, they associated two other Jansenist bishops with him, those of Haarlem and Deventer. This Jansenist Church has now three bishops, some thirty priests and about ten thousand faithful.

Jansenism also found adherents in Italy. They were chiefly sympathizers, enemies of the Jesuits and partisans of the State authority in religious matters; among them may be mentioned Cardinal Noris, Fulgentius Belelli, Lorenzo Berti, Cardinal Passionei, Tamburini, Zola, Serrao, G. Capecelatro, etc. The best known was Scipio de Ricci, who held a synod at Pistoia in 1786; its decrees were condemned by the Bull *Auctorem fidei* of Pius VI in 1794, and this gave the *coup de grâce* to Italian Jansenism.

CHAPTER IX

HERESIES FROM THE SEVENTEENTH TO THE TWENTIETH CENTURY

The human soul is fated nearly always to trace a path between two chasms, two extremes, two dangers: when it casts itself upon God to the point of desiring to be lost in him this is often demoralizing Quietism, and when it keeps at a distance from God, trusting only in its own reason and instinct, this is naturalism, far more common and more dangerous than Quietism. Already in every chapter of this book these two dangers could be pointed to; they are the two perpetual temptations of the human mind. In fact we have done this by dividing the Protestant sects between rationalism and illuminism. It will be much more evident in the course of the present chapter dealing with modern and contemporary errors or heresies in the universal Church.

QUIETISM

As has just been said, Quietism is not something entirely modern; in fact it has already appeared many times in the course of the centuries, very often accompanied by suspect doctrines or immoral practices. It may be defined as "the quest for an extreme spiritual passivity tending to the destruction of the human self through absorption in God". Understood thus, Quietism is at the root of Buddhism, whose ideal is *nirvana*. It is found again in neo-platonic ecstasy.[1]

Confining our attention to Christian spirituality, we can note that there had been Quietism among the Messalians or Euchites condemned by the Council of Ephesus in 431; they thought to reach perpetual peace in the war against the demons by means of continuous prayer. Traces are again found in the Hesychasts of the fourteenth century, in the monasteries of Mount Athos, and in the west among the Fraticelli, Beghards and Béguines in the thirteenth century, who aspired to sinlessness through absorption in God, and were condemned at the Council of Vienne in 1312. Quietism is also to be discerned in the teaching of Master Eckhart, twenty-eight of whose propositions were condemned by John XXII in 1329. Quietism was also the principal error of the Spanish *Alumbrados* of the sixteenth and seventeenth centuries, who were constantly harried by the Inquisition.

The most complete theorist of Quietism was the Spanish priest, Miguel de Molinos, who was born at Munies near Saragossa in 1628 and died at Rome in 1696. He was a man of depth of character, devout and of gentle disposition, pleasing and attractive, with a highly intelligent mind and widely cultured. He came to Rome to further a cause for beatification and was unwilling to leave the city of the popes. He quickly made himself known and was reputed as a director of souls. His chief work was a book written in Spanish, *The Spiritual Guide*, which appeared in Rome in 1675. This work was particularly admired by German Protestant Pietists, who translated it into German and Latin. Molinos taught that Christian perfection consists in the perfect quietude of the soul; this quietude must extend to the suppression of all desire, including the desire for sanctity and, with greater

[1] Quietism may be compared with certain forms of Gnosticism.

reason, the desire for heaven. In this state of complete quietude the soul is annihilated in God, lost in absolute abandon to his good pleasure, and it need no longer guard against evil thoughts and desires, or even immoral actions, which might trouble it. In fact these are no longer sins for such a soul; its will, absorbed in God, does not consent to them; on the contrary, the best way of annihilating itself is to accept these temptations and sensual deviations without in the least concerning itself about them.

The first to denounce these errors was the celebrated Italian preacher, Segneri, the "Italian Bourdaloue", also a Jesuit. But so popular were these ideas that at first Segneri was blamed for his criticism. Yet when the writings of Molinos were subjected to close scrutiny and especially when the 20,000-odd letters of direction in which he set forth his most intimate thoughts became known, the full extent of the evil was appreciated. In the convents of which he was director the nuns thought lightly of confession, indulgences, penance and vocal prayer, and regarded themselves as not blame-worthy for their material faults. Sixty-eight propositions extracted from Molinos' works were condemned by Innocent XI on November 20th, 1687. Molinos had been arrested in 1685; he was condemned to perpetual detention, retracted his errors in 1687 and died only nine years later.

SEMI-QUIETISM

An attenuated form of the same teaching developed in France soon afterwards and involved in conflict the two leading personages of the national clergy, Bossuet and Fénelon. A certain widow, Madame Guyon (née Jeanne-Marie Bouvier de la Motte), born at Montargis in 1648, after her husband's death had become extremely devout and placed herself under the direction of the Barnabite Fr François Lacombe, ecclesiastical superior of the Ursulines of Thonon. Now Fr Lacombe was a Quietist. Mme Guyon adopted his theories with enthusiasm and published vehement and obscure works in which she exhibited them as the very doctrine of perfection for all men. *Les Torrents spirituels* ("Spiritual Torrents"), *Le Moyen court et très facile de faire oraison* ("The Short and Easy Method of Prayer") and *Le Cantique des Cantiques* ("The Song of Songs"). After Molinos' condemnation, Fr Lacombe was himself the object of investigation, was arrested, questioned and shut up in the Bastille in 1687. He died in 1699 in the lunatic asylum at Charenton. Mme Guyon was likewise interned for a time in an Ursuline convent (1688), but on her release gained the support of three great ladies, among them Mme de Maintenon, and even obtained the approval of Fénelon, then tutor to the Duke of Burgundy. Her theories, discussed with incredible subtlety by Fénelon and Bossuet in the long series of the *Conférences d'Issy* (1694–5), led to a document of thirty-four articles which Mme Guyon and Fénelon signed, as well as Bossuet and his friends. But when Bossuet produced a commentary on them in a book called *Les États d'Oraison* ("States of Prayer") Fénelon replied with his "Explanations of the Maxims of the Saints", striking rather a different note. The book was delated to the Holy See, which condemned twenty-three of its propositions on March 12th, 1699. Fénelon immediately submitted unreservedly. The first proposition contains the essence of this dangerous teaching: "There is a habitual state of love of God which is pure charity unmixed with any self-interest. Neither fear of penalties nor desire for reward has any part in it. We love God no longer with the idea of meriting or of attaining perfection, nor in order to obtain the happiness which we find through loving him." This meant that "pure love" demands a complete disappropriation and the suppression of those acts of hope to which the Church obliges Christians.

We may add that neither Fr Lacombe nor Mme Guyon, nor *a fortiori* the sensitive and refined Fénelon, had ever laid

themselves open to the charge of moral indifferentism which
had been brought against Molinos.

NATURALISM

The contrary of Quietism, which is a heresy for the very
élite among souls, is Naturalism. It may be said that this is
the great heresy of modern times. Here only a very limited
account of it can be given, but the names which we shall
mention amongst the many are so well-known either in the
history of contemporary modern philosophy or in literary
history that each of them will constitute sufficient indication.

First, then. what is Naturalism? It is denial of the supernatural, of divine revelation, of all positive religion, such as
Christianity, of the miraculous, even of its possibility, of all
binding and infallible dogma. In Naturalism it is man, human
reason, human conscience and human passions according to
the point of view, which replace revealed religion. The very
law of Naturalism is this sort of anarchy of ideas and systems
which has characterized contemporary modern society since
the eighteenth century. As some sort of guide in the heart of
this anarchy we here consider it under subtitles which are in
fact only varieties of Naturalism in general.

FREE-THOUGHT

The word free-thinker, which was to have such a strange
career, appeared for the first time in a letter from Molyneux
to John Locke, concerning an Irish apostate, John Toland,
who had just published a book called *Christianity not
Mysterious*, in which he professed an integral rationalism.
But before Toland, there can be quoted Herbert of Cherbury,
Hobbes, John Locke and Shaftesbury, and it can be clearly
seen how free-thought arose from the disgust caused by the
unending theological quarrels between Protestants and
Catholics and still more between Protestant sects, particularly

English Episcopalians and Presbyterians. Among the free-thinkers in England may be cited Collins, Tindal and Lord Bolingbroke, one of Voltaire's masters. The titles of some of the works which they published are revealing: "Discourse on Freedom of Thought" (Collins, 1713), "The Rights of the Christian Church defended against Roman Priests" (Tindal, 1706), "Christianity as old as Creation" (idem., 1730), "Thoughts on Natural Religion" (Bolingbroke, 1736).

But the real arsenal of free-thought was the *Dictionnaire historique et critique* (Historical and critical dictionary) of Pierre Bayle (1647–1706), who had been by turns Protestant, then Catholic, then Protestant again and finally a free-thinker. This Dictionary, prodigiously erudite for the times and apparently orthodox, was an inexhaustible mine of doubt, objections and critical reflections against the dogmas and traditions of Christianity. Published in 1697, it ran into more than ten editions before 1760, and possibly provided the primary inspiration for the Encyclopedia.

Bayle was of French origin, and it was in France that free-thought, although nourished by the English writers named above, developed with lightning-like rapidity in the eighteenth century. But a simple enumeration of names and works must suffice here; until 1750 free-thought was confined to elegant satire, and there is still no trace of anger. It remains at the stage of facile mockery, and criticism of beliefs and institutions. The great enemy of tradition is Montesquieu of the *Lettres Persanes* (1721), but soon Voltaire enters the scene; he is a ready writer, piquant, light, witty, avid for fame, luxury, enjoyment, dealing with everything, laughing at everything and having respect for none.

But after 1750 a second period begins in which implacable hatred against revealed religion makes its appearance. Over and over again the keynote is to be found in Voltaire's letters to his friends—"Let us crush the Beast!" (*Ecrasons l'infâme!*). The most formidable engine of war arrayed against the Christian faith and the Church is the "Encyclopedia or analytical

Dictionary of sciences, arts and measures, by a Society of Men of Letters", prospectus in 1750, Volume I in 1751, publication ended 1766, 17 folio volumes with five supplementary volumes in 1777, and 11 volumes of plates). Two men, Diderot and d'Alembert, directed the publication, but all the important writers of the century collaborated—Voltaire, Montesquieu, Buffon, Condillac, Mably, Turgot, Helvétius, d'Holbach, Marmontel, Grimm and Necker.

ROUSSEAU

In this picture of free-thought, an original and eloquent writer, Jean-Jacques Rousseau, must be considered separately; he was moving, attractive, colourful and romantic, always holding aloof from the writers of his time. With him we are at the very centre of naturalism. He glorifies nature, proclaiming it to be pure and good in itself and in its origins. He certainly would never admit original sin. With Rousseau we are at the opposite pole from Lutheranism, Calvinism and Jansenism. It is society that has corrupted man and the arts and sciences have only aggravated human corruption. Based on this paradox—we may ask how man, who is fundamentally good, could become corrupted in common—Rousseau founded a sort of new religion, taking the form of romanticism in literature, but which is the foundation of the present religion of progress, science and technique. With Rousseau this religion is worship of nature, of its instincts, sentiments, passionate impulses, in short the worship of the human heart, and still more of human reason. The *Confessions* (which appeared in 1781), *La Nouvelle Héloïse* (1761), *Émile* (1762), the *Social Contract* (1762), of which the Revolution made a sort of Gospel, exercised an immeasurable influence. Rousseau can be regarded as the father of the democratic mysticism which inspired Marat, Robespierre, and later, Edgar Quinet and the neo-Jacobins of Combism—and he is equally the father of the socialist and communist mysticism which by way of Saint-Simon, Fourier, Proudhon and Karl Marx led to Jaurès, Léon Blum, on the one hand, and to Lenin and Stalin on the other. Lastly, Rousseau is the father of passionate and aesthetic mysticism, which has been the inspiration not only of contemporary literature but also of the religion of music or art for art's sake.

AGNOSTICISM AND POSITIVISM

Naturalism, whose development we have tried to describe, has also penetrated the realm of philosophy. Descartes, in his rectilinear rationalism, kept a place for revealed religion, but after him Locke (1632–1704) turned his ideas in a positivist direction. David Hume (1711–76) accentuated this tendency. Emmanuel Kant (1724–1804) tended to agnosticism by holding in the *Critique of Pure Reason* the incapacity of human reason in the face of the absolute. Man, according to Kant, can prove nothing about God, the soul, moral liberty or the substance of things. Nevertheless, the moral law, written in the heart of man, postulates the existence of God. So Kant maintains natural religion, not revealed religion, by virtue of an unprovable postulate, of a requirement of conscience and, in a word, subjective belief. But he allows no other revelation than that which man makes to himself, and he foretells a new era when the "humiliating distinction between laity and clergy will disappear of its own accord".

After Kant and Fichte and then Hegel, philosophy pays particular attention to the identification of religion and progress, religion and rising evolution. God does not exist but is in process of coming into being in and through man. God is the secret ideal to which human evolution is tending.

Analogous ideas were held in France, in a very different form, by Auguste Comte, the father of Positivism. For him God, the soul and substance were words devoid of meaning, creations of the human mind in its first gropings. Only one thing is attainable by us—that which is reached through the

senses or through scientific observation. Theology must give
way to philosophy and philosophy shut itself up in the pursuit of science. Auguste Comte is the father of scientism, of
which Renan was to be the herald in his book *L'Avenir de la
Science* ("The Future of Science"). But this leads us to an
important investigation, that of the laws of diffusion of contemporary naturalism.

THE LAWS OF DIFFUSION

In the eighteenth century, as in the nineteenth, there was to
be discerned a curious law of diffusion for naturalist anti-
religious ideas. This law is analogous to that of the gradual
loss of energy in the physical sphere. Diffusion takes place in
three stages, in the course of which the idea is continuously
subject to a process of loss of its original purity. In the first
stage the doctrine is confined to lofty philosophical spheres;
it retains a certain serenity. Its denials are categorical and
formal, but also theoretical and courteous, often even respectful. John Locke's Positivism at the beginning of the eighteenth
century, and Auguste Comte's in the middle of the nineteenth,
are not aggressive in tone. They are, rather, discussions of
pure ideas.

In the second stage, these ideas fall like oracles on minds
that are less powerful, original and profound, but more
daring and more hasty, which hurry to publicize them in
stark, unqualified assertions. Voltaire in the eighteenth century and Renan in the nineteenth perform the same function
for the lone thinkers of their times. Their limpid and lively
style, their talent for exposition and expression, serve the
cause which they have embraced in a marvellous manner.
Renan makes Hegelianism accessible and attractive. In the
wake of these publicizers of genius gathers a host of disciples,
fanatical and enthusiastic partisans—lecturers, pamphleteers,
journalists, novelists, professors and politicians. Passing from
mouth to mouth, the teachings become deformed and imbued

with instinctive tendencies to violence and stubbornness which takes the place of proofs. The world of fashion takes up the ideas and public opinion is influenced.

Finally, in the third stage, anti-religious theories—scientism, materialism and Marxism—reach the people. Here they are transformed into entirely primitive passions. Discussion of ideas becomes discussion of interests, personal opposition and party political struggles. Scientism becomes anti-clericalism, and hate makes its appearance. Racism and class warfare, the great battle between communism and capitalism, flourish amid these frantic passions. Disorder and disunity among Christians—for the most part the participants are baptized and therefore Christians—reach their height. The downward trend of ideas is striking; from books to newspapers and from newspapers to the mob. Naturalism thus reaches a point that its initiators had been unable to foresee, that of the complete demoralization of the masses, with increase of crime and social anarchy, and in reaction, totalitarianism either of State or Party; and that is where we are.

It will be recalled that a catalogue of modern naturalist errors, drawn up and published on December 8th, 1864, by Pius IX, under the name of the Syllabus, aroused almost unbelievable anger, even among statesmen, and above all among publicists and their regular readers. This denunciation of errors was itself denounced as evidence of obscurantism and a retrograde spirit, but the Church has nothing to withdraw of her former condemnations which were only too justified.

AMERICANISM

In including Americanism among heresies, we are doing so merely to record its existence, for it was not in fact a formal heresy but at the most a passing naturalistic infection which must needs disappear as soon as it had been denounced and condemned.

The facts are as follows. Among the leading Catholic missionaries in America was Fr Isaac Thomas Hecker, founder of the "Missionaries of St Paul" (or Paulists). Born in New York in 1819, of Protestant parents, he was converted to Catholicism in 1844, joined the Redemptorists a year later and was ordained priest in 1849. On returning to America he made a great reputation as a preacher, but at an early stage he seems to have put forward ideas which the Church was to condemn under the name of "Americanism".

Fr Hecker, in disagreement with the Redemptorists, left them to found a new congregation which grew rapidly. He died in 1888 and was remembered as a zealous man, a true apostle who had grasped the necessity in missionary work of making use of the most modern methods of our times, notably the press. Thus a congregation under the patronage of St Paul came into being, and was fully approved during this present century, that places in the front rank of its missionary method the use of modern devices such as the press, the cinema and television, but more especially the press. It was not this which caused the condemnation of Americanism, but Fr Hecker had been posthumously commemorated by an imprudent biographer, Fr Elliott, whose book, published in 1894, was translated into French in 1897. Abbé Charles Maignen denounced it in a pamphlet entitled "Is Fr Hecker a saint?" A lively controversy ensued, which resulted in the condemnation of Americanism.

What are we to understand by the term? In the first place it is a tendency to belittle the traditional constitution of the Church on the grounds that "the future is with the democracies", and that the word freedom henceforth exerts a magic influence on the mind. The Church somehow or other must cease to be a religion of authority and must become, like Protestantism, a religion of freedom.

In the second place, according to the exponents of Americanism, it is time to revise the scale of spiritual values. The Middle Ages extolled the passive virtues, humility, obedience, poverty, mortification, etc.; our era, according to the Americanists, rightly esteems the active virtues as being much more important, vigorous action, an external apostolate, conducted by oral discussion and in the press, and by means of modern publicity techniques—in short, by every method which can be described as up-to-date; a dynamic approach in order to enforce the triumph of truth and justice! Men of action are masters of the world.

With such aspirations we are evidently confronted with the opposite extreme to Quietism, outlined at the beginning of this chapter. For this reason, ideas of this sort are today given the name of Activism, since they represent the exact opposite of Quietism. The Church accepts neither of these positions; Leo XIII, who was certainly entitled to be called a dynamic pope, condemned Americanism outright in his letter *Testem benevolentiae*, addressed to Cardinal Gibbons on January 22nd, 1899. But Activism, a renewed form of Americanism, remains a temptation and indeed a danger for the Church even at the present time.

MODERNISM

And it is the same, though far more seriously, with Modernism, with which we propose to end this short history of heresy. In his Encyclical *Humani generis*, of August 12th, 1950, Pius XII referred to the dangers of Modernism under the new forms in which it has sought to clothe itself in our time. Here we confine ourselves to the Modernism of fifty years ago, condemned by St Pius X in his Encyclical *Pascendi* of September 8th, 1907.

It is a fact, which may be observed throughout this book, that between Catholic orthodoxy and the prevailing heresy of the period attempts, illusory for the most part, have always been made to compromise, to reconcile or adapt, if possible, immutable Catholic truth with the changing mentality of the centuries. The Modernism denounced in the Encyclical *Humani generis* is the most recent example of this. That condemned in 1907 was also an attempt of this sort, and it is permissible to call it semi-naturalism. It made its appearance in the last years of the nineteenth century, in several places at the same time, but only in university circles and among ecclesiastics of advanced scientific attainments. In France the chief initiator of Modernism was a priest, Alfred Loisy, a learned exegetist and professor at the Catholic Institute of Paris, who, in order the better to combat the liberal Protestantism of men like Adolf Harnack and his kind, as he said, completely adopted the terminology and methods of his opponents. During 1902 he published a little book called *L'Évangile et l'Église* ("The Gospel and the Church"), in which the latest ideas were discreetly and cleverly put forward. According to him, the Gospel originated at a time when the end of the world was considered to be near, and appeared with eschatological preoccupations. Then, as the end of the world did not come, the Church was established as mistress among Christian people who saw the destiny of the earth extended beyond the foreseen period. Thus, all Christianity was reduced to a kind of illusory Adventism. When critics arose on all sides against this daring theory, Alfred Loisy asserted his views in a second work which was entitled *Autour d'un petit livre* (1903). At this point it was obvious that behind his theory there was a special philosophy of the history of dogma. A small number of voices, but each one of some authority, soon echoed his own: Tyrrell, the ex-Jesuit in England, Hermann Schell at Würzburg in Germany, Buonaiutti, Murri, Menocchi, the novelist Fogazzaro in Italy. All held ideas more or less related to those of Abbé Loisy.

What made the refutation of this heresy particularly difficult was that it represented a state of mind, fleeting and ill-defined tendencies rather than a body of determined doctrine. At Rome, however, a patient and searching inquiry was begun. A list of sixty-five propositions drawn from the work of various suspect authors was compiled. These were condemned in the decree *Lamentabili*, of July 3rd, 1907. Then, without

pausing, Pius X began preparation of a more elaborate
document, giving a complete description of the state of soul
constituting what the pope was the first to label Modernism.
This was the Encyclical *Pascendi*, so strongly framed and
containing such a strikingly drawn portrait of total Modernism
that the authors concerned were themselves stupefied. The
pope however named no one and simply drew this pen-picture
of the modernist successively as philosopher, believer, theologian, critic, apologist and reformer.

As a philosopher, the modernist lays down as the first
principle that we know nothing about God, either of his
existence or his attributes, through intellectual reasoning.
Thus he takes as his starting-point Kantian and Positivist
agnosticism. Religion, that is, belief in God, is for him a
spontaneous and irrational product of our nature. God is revealed to us, in the depths of the heart, by the demands of our
moral conscience, by the instinctive feelings of our soul which
needs an ideal in order to live. This interior appeal is what
is called immanentism.

As a believer, the modernist clings to this God revealed to
him by his conscience, he looks at him, in the name of his
interior experience, as truly real although indemonstrable, and
for the barrenness of atheistic rationalism he substitutes a
tender though purely subjective mysticism. The Pietists had
done the same, and Schleiermacher had reached the same
conclusion; he was a Protestant theologian (1768–1834) who
had restored belief which had almost been destroyed by the
rationalism of the eighteenth-century philosophers.

As a theologian, the modernist describes the unconscious
work which the soul of the believer accomplishes in seeking
to think his faith. He is obliged of course to appeal to the
ideas of his times. Thus he invents formulas which pass from
mouth to mouth and, becoming traditional, crystallize in the
struggle against inevitable opposition. In this way dogmas
arise. And with the dogmas, sustaining them, are rites. But,
concludes the modernist, on reflection dogmas or rites—which

have become sacraments—can only have been the occasional vehicles of belief, and can have no other value beyond that of symbols of this belief; they can and must disappear when the religious sense, having grown adult and conscious, no longer has need of them.

As a historian, the modernist affects to believe only in texts, sources and evidence. But, not forgetting that he is also a philosopher and a theologian, he sifts the texts in such a way as to bring them into agreement with his own philosophical and theological systems. Thus he declares that the miraculous is unthinkable and expunges from the texts whatever is supernatural in them. He will compile, he says, a critical and scientific history. It is in this way that Alfred Loisy treats the Gospel, just as Anatole France treated Joan of Arc and the novelist Zola the events of Lourdes.

Armed with this history, the modernist still thinks that he can set himself up as an apologist for religion, he appeals to the rationalists and shows them Catholicism reconciled in his person with the modern mentality and with modern science. He thinks that he is in a position to sign an alliance between the Church and free-thought. But he is well aware that reform comes from within and that is why he insists on remaining in the Church, since at heart he feels that he is separated from her by a whole world of opinions and theories which that Church rejects with horror.

Following the condemnation of Modernism by St Pius X, the modernists were obliged to exclude themselves from the Church. Like other heresies, Modernism produced a useful result. It began a return to sources—sometimes called *ressourcement*—which was manifested by a splendid renewal of biblical and patristic studies, an almost general liturgical revival whose effects are experienced in parish life by the participation of the faithful in the sacred mysteries, in a deeper knowledge of religion and in a great desire for instruction in this matter.

Even in the dissident Christian sects this movement spread

with greater or less intensity. A theologian like Karl Barth, in the very heart of Calvinism, must be considered an anti-modernist. He too desired to return to sources. He took as centre the person of Jesus Christ, immolated and abased for love of us. From the Catholic point of view, it must be regretted that he has remained in strict Calvinism, but what must be unreservedly praised is his desire for pure Gospel preaching and a Christian life in as perfect conformity as possible with the ideal of evangelical charity.

It is only remotely that two forms of thought of completely opposite tendencies, which appeared in France, can be connected with Modernism; Mark Sangnier's "Sillon" on the one hand and Charles Maurras' "Action française" on the other. Both movements were concerned to link the Church with a political conception, to democracy in the case of the "Sillon" and to traditional monarchy in that of the "Action française". The two movements were successively condemned in the name of the supra-political character of the Church. It cannot be denied too frequently that Charles Maurras showed his external adherence to Catholicism in a strongly anti-evangelical, and therefore unchristian light. But these were only passing errors; correction was required and was administered and that was the end of the matter.

CHAPTER X

CONCLUSION: WILL ECUMENICALISM PUT AN END TO HERESY?

THIRST FOR UNITY

One of the most imposing and significant religious events of the last half-century is the appearance and development of ecumenicalism, the name given to that powerful movement which is working for the restoration of Christian unity.

For too long Christianity has presented a divided face to the world. Jesus Christ, in his "priestly prayer" at the Last Supper, prayed for the unity of his disciples and gave this same unity as one of the signs by which the world might recognize that he had been sent by the Father. So nothing was more unchristian than the disunity of the Churches. Already it is a gain of first importance for these Churches that they have recovered the desire for if not yet the secret of unity. They have learnt to respect rather than to fight one another, to confer calmly and peaceably on the best means of becoming reconciled, and above all to pray in common in order to obtain from God that grace which is the mark of unity.

Clearly we cannot hope for a positive result in a short time. The gulf made by four centuries of division cannot be healed quickly without a real miracle, but it is already a great achievement that conversations have begun to take place, either in important meetings or in friendly private discussions between "separated brethren".

This thirst for unity and this undeniable brotherhood already form one effective remedy for the all too regrettable dissensions of the past and some reparation for the scandal caused to non-Christians all over the world.

HISTORICAL SURVEY

Ecumenical conferences were inaugurated on the initiative of a group of Protestant missionaries. The first of these meetings, which can be regarded as the birth of contemporary ecumenicalism, took place at Edinburgh in 1910. It was thought more prudent not to enter into doctrinal discussions to start with, and the conference was concerned merely with the question of setting up "world-wide missionary conferences". A second meeting, which took place at Stockholm in 1925, was called the "Conference of Life and Action". It dealt with scarcely anything but social questions, but the undeniable success of these first two meetings led to the summoning of a "Conference of Faith and Order" at Lausanne in 1927. There the thorny problem of doctrines was at last broached, and two tendencies were revealed, "Life and Action" on the one hand and "Faith and Order" on the other. The former paid more attention to practice than to dogma while the latter was concerned with the Creed and its contents. The two sections held separate meetings in 1937, the first at Oxford, the second at Edinburgh.

An important step forward was then made. The two sections, instead of confronting and opposing each other, resolved to amalgamate and together it was decided to found what was called the "World Council of Churches". The war postponed the carrying out of this great project but it was not forgotten. The Pan-Christian assembly took place at Amsterdam from

August 22nd to September 4th, 1948. There the World Council of Churches, which had been projected in 1937, was founded under that title (W.C.C.). This Council was still world-wide only in intention. All-important Churches were still missing; in the first place, for reasons which we shall see presently, the Roman Catholic Church, which alone contains more baptized persons than all the others together—430 million out of a total of 790 million, of whom 200 million are Orthodox and 160 million are Protestants of various denominations—abstained entirely while showing the keenest interest in this moving desire manifested by the meeting. Among the oriental Churches (the Orthodox), the Russian Church expressly refused to take part. Among the Protestant Churches, the Unitarians or anti-Trinitarian Churches were not admitted, and some important groups such as the Baptists of the southern United States, the Lutherans of Missouri, etc., held aloof. It must also be noted that all those small sects which we have mentioned above as being less in their numerical adherents than in the virulence of their propaganda showed themselves violently hostile to any *rapprochement* and to the ecumenical movement itself.

This Amsterdam conference was of great interest none the less. Its avowed purpose was recovery of the *Una Sancta*, that is, the Church of Christ, one and holy. Serious difficulties appeared. The shrewd and "irenic" secretary of the meeting, W. A. Wisser't Hooft, had the courage to disclose the gravity and immensity of the problem: "We all believe," he said, "that a Church exists within the Churches, but we are not agreed as to how its exists or where it exists, neither on how or where it may be realized." And again: "The Ecumenical Council must not claim to represent the *Una Sancta*, but it can and it must proclaim that a body does exist in which and by which, when God pleases, the *Una Sancta* will be made manifest."

Four hundred official delegates were present at this meeting, representing 150 Churches, and about three thousand people, that is, all that the *Niewe Kerk* (New Church) of Amsterdam would hold.

The general subject debated was thus formulated: "Man's Disorder and God's Plan, that is, the duties and possibilities of the Church in the face of disordered humanity." The discussions passed off peacefully in spite of a few untoward incidents—Foster Dulles' outburst against communism, the Czechoslovakian Hromadka's against capitalism, and the Calvinist theologian Karl Barth's public and private diatribes against the Catholic Church.

Although generally speaking discussion was calm and dignified, regretfully it must be stated that the Churches meeting together could not celebrate the Lord's Supper together. On a point of capital importance division remained glaring. The Churches were obliged to declare that they possessed unity of doctrine on neither the priesthood, the sacraments nor the Church herself and her visible Head. They felt united only in their common veneration of the Saviour Christ.

The second assembly of the World Council of Churches was held from August 15th–31st, 1954, in the United States. There 1,298 persons took part, in the following categories: 502 delegates, 499 accredited visitors, 145 consultants, 96 young consultants, 31 "fraternal delegates" and 25 observers. These participants came from 179 Churches drawn from 54 countries. The delegates properly so called represented 162 member-Churches of the World Council in 42 countries. The central theme, adopted at the preparatory meetings of the permanent central committee in 1950, 1951 and 1953, was "Christ, the hope of the world". Apart from the Catholic Church, the principal denominations not represented at Evanston were the Lutheran Synod of Missouri, the Baptist Church of the South and the Patriarchate of Moscow. Once again, after the formal reports given to the meeting and fraternal and amicable discussions, the Council was obliged to acknowledge that progress towards unity was still far from sufficient. "We are now entering on the second stage of the movement," said the final declaration, "remaining together is not enough; we must advance. In proportion as we are better acquainted with our unity in Christ, our divisions become the more intolerable." Again the general communion at the Lord's Supper had to be abandoned.

It may be asked why the Catholic Church remains outside this movement which in many ways is so praiseworthy and moving. Explanation of this point shall form the conclusion of this book.

THE ROMAN CATHOLIC CHURCH, CENTRE OF UNITY

The whole of this present book is proof on the one hand of the antiquity[1] of the Catholic, Apostolic and Roman Church, and on the other of the constant assistance of the Holy Spirit, with which she has been favoured according to the formal promise of her founder, Jesus Christ. Without this marvellous continuity of the Catholic Church, there would have been no Christianity for many centuries past. From Gnosticism, fertile in error of all kinds, down to multiform and all-embracing naturalism, by way of every kind of variety of Protestantism, the true faith would long since have vanished, without the authority of the Church and her continual corrective action down the ages. But precisely because of this great past, and above all because of the deep and ardent certainty possessed by all Catholics that the Christian rule of faith could not have been maintained intact in its life-giving power, nor have undergone the legitimate and harmonious developments that this very vitality imposes on it, without the assistance of the Holy Spirit, it is impossible to submit the sacred deposit of the faith, received from the Church's Master, Jesus Christ, to negotiation, discussion or compromise, with the risk of altera-

[1] A Lutheran could also speak of antiquity, but he would be obliged to do so *via* the Catholic Church. The point of rupture remains in the sixteenth century.

tion, nor yet allow discussion of her immortal rights and pre-
rogatives, as in a parliamentary assembly.

Christian unity is the foremost concern of a Catholic. There
is no sincere believer who remains unmoved by the great
thirst for unity manifested in the ecumenical movement. The
members of the World Council of Churches are aware of this.
M. Marc Boegner, president of the Federation of Protestant
Churches of France, and a convinced ecumenicalist, said this
very well in the Paris newspaper *Figaro* on August 9th, 1954:
"The Roman Church," he wrote, "inexorably maintains
against other Christian confessions that she is the only true
Church of Christ. Hence it is in her alone that Christian unity
can be restored. And at the same time a growing number of
her priests, religious and faithful, associate themselves by
prayer and study with the great work which for almost half
a century has been seeking to remove the scandal of the
divisions of the Church. . . ."

The Catholic Church has thus no difficulty in closely combining the passionate desire for Christian unity and the certainty that this unity is only possible in the unity of faith,
communion and government that she has always preserved
through nineteen centuries. This unity is not only her dearest
treasure but is the sacred property of the Holy Spirit, who
has willed it and protected it, and forms the only hope of
mankind. Perhaps one day the Catholic Church will take
part in an ecumenical assembly, if she is given the presidency
and if to begin with her divine right of directing the universal
Church is recognized. And that is obviously the meaning of
this declaration by Cardinal Stritch, Archbishop of Chicago,
concerning the Assembly at Evanston: "The Catholic Church
can take no part in any organization in which the delegates
of numerous sects gather in council or conference to discuss
on an equal footing the subject of the nature of the Church
of Christ or of the nature of her unity."

Benedict XV had previously defined the unchanging position of the Roman Church towards ecumenicalism. As he

had been invited to a Congress of the kind here mentioned, he explained the attitude of Rome in these words: "His Holiness . . . does not in any way wish to disapprove of the Congress in question for those who are not in union with the Chair of Peter; on the contrary, he very much desires and prays that, if the Congress takes place, those who take part may by God's grace see the light and become reunited to the visible Head of the Church, who will receive them with open arms."

No other attitude is possible, for any abandonment of Catholic dogma would be treachery, apostasy and consequently destruction of the hope which humanity must place in its only Saviour who is Christ. The infinite love of God has not left the redemptive message to the free discussions of men. It has entrusted it to a Church which represents it, in which it lives, from whence it teaches. It has given this Church visible marks to make her known to all honest and sincere minds. St Augustine gives a succinct statement of these marks in the following sentence from one of his sermons: "How was the Church of God, which is to be spread among the nations, foretold? She is one, built upon the Rock, and such that the gates of hell cannot prevail against her." As never before there must be fervent prayer for unity in all the Churches.

SELECT BIBLIOGRAPHY

BEDOYERE, Michael de la: *The Life of Baron von Hügel*, London, Dent, and New York, Scribners, 1951.

HUGHES, Philip: *The Reformation in England*, three volumes, London, Hollis and Carter, and New York, Macmillan, 1950–4.

HUGHES, Philip: *History of the Church*, London and New York, Sheed and Ward, 1947.

KNOX, R. A.: *Enthusiasm, A Chapter in the History of Religion with special Reference to the Seventeenth and Eighteenth Centuries*, Oxford and New York, Oxford Univ. Press, 1950.

LEBRETON, Jules, S.J.: *The Life and Teaching of Jesus Christ*, London, Burns Oates, and New York, Macmillan, 1958.

LEBRETON, Jules, S.J., and ZEILLER, Jacques: *The History of the Primitive Church*, four volumes, London, Burns Oates, 1942–8, and New York, Macmillan.

MANN, H. K., and HOLLNSTEINER, J.: *The Lives of the Popes in the Middle Ages*, eighteen volumes, London, Kegan Paul, and St Louis, Herder, 1928–32.

MAY, J. Lewis: *Father Tyrrell and the Modernist Movement*, London, Eyre and Spottiswoode, 1932.

PASTOR, Ludwig von: *The History of the Popes from the Close of the Middle Ages,* London, Kegan Paul, and St Louis, Herder, 1937–40.

POURRAT, Pierre, S.S.: *Christian Spirituality*, Volume IV (From Jansenism to Modern Times), translated by Donald Attwater, Westminster, Md, Newman Press, 1955.

TODD, John M.: *Catholicism and the Ecumenical Movement*, London and New York, Longmans, 1956; *John Wesley and the Catholic Church*, London, Hodder and Stoughton, and New York, Macmillan, 1958.

The Twentieth Century Encyclopedia of Catholicism

The number of each volume indicates its place in the over-all series and not the order of appearance.

TWENTIETH CENTURY ENCYCLOPEDIA OF CATHOLICISM

All titles are subject to change.

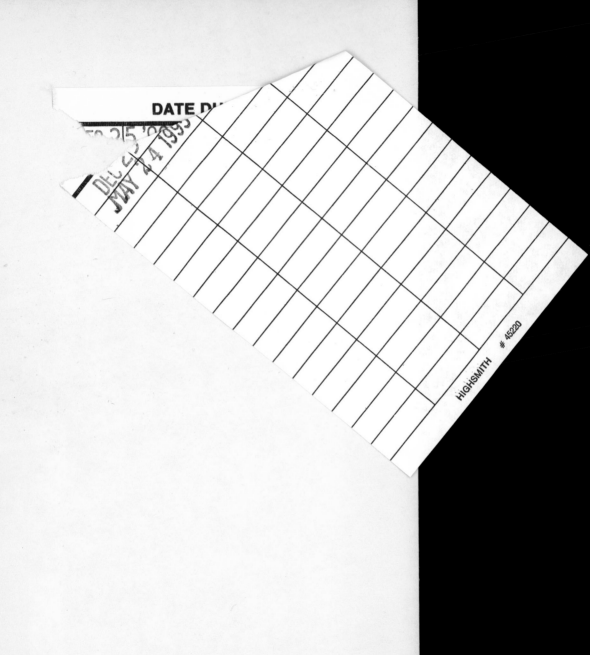

DATE DUE

DEC 2 5
MAY 2 4 1995

HIGHSMITH   # 45220